How to Invest for Beginners

HOW TO INVEST FOR BEGINNERS

Stock Market Investing

Simple Bond Investing

The Truth About Investing for Beginners

What No One Tells You

by

John King
Expert in Investing

"The stock market is a device for transferring money from the impatient to the patient." – ***Warren Buffett***

"Risk comes from not knowing what you're doing." – ***Warren Buffett***

4.*"The biggest risk of all is not taking one."* – ***Mellody Hobson***

5.*"In investing, what is comfortable is rarely profitable."* – ***Robert Arnott***

Introduction

Investing is one of the most powerful ways to grow wealth over time, but it can also feel overwhelming for beginners. Whether you're considering the stock market, bonds, or other investment options, understanding the risks, rewards, and strategies is key to making informed decisions.

Unlike a savings account—where your money earns minimal interest but remains safe—investing in stocks and bonds offers the potential for higher returns, along with greater risks. Many young adults are entering the market earlier than previous generations, yet barriers like lack of knowledge, fear of risk, and limited funds can hold them back.

This guide explores essential investing questions, from how the stock market differs from a savings account to the risks and rewards of bonds. You'll learn why timing the market is so difficult, how speculative investing can lead to instability, and practical steps to start building your portfolio. By the end, you'll have a clearer understanding of how investing works and how to make smarter financial choices for your future.

Let's dive in!

Chapter 1

The Truth About Investing for Beginners – What No One Tells You

Smart, Capable, and Still Stuck

If you've ever felt paralyzed by the idea of investing—even though you *know* it's important—you're not alone. Every day, highly educated people with thriving careers and complex problem-solving skills avoid taking even the simplest financial steps.

They read. They watch. They listen. And yet—they don't act.

Why? Because the world of money is wired to trigger fear, shame, and confusion. It's not a matter of intelligence. It's a psychological minefield that exploits even the most rational minds.

This is the Beginner's Trap.

In this investigation, we'll explore the emotional, neurological, and behavioral forces that keep smart people from building wealth—and the surprisingly simple systems that can finally unlock financial momentum.

Section 1: The Psychology of Financial Avoidance

The Paralysis Paradox: Why Smart People Don't Invest

In a 2023 Vanguard study of 10,000 educated professionals—including doctors, engineers, and lawyers—researchers found something shocking:

- **68%** of respondents could accurately explain compound interest.
- Yet **73%** were keeping over **$50,000** in low-yield savings accounts earning less than **1%** annually.

These are people who make life-and-death decisions in hospitals, design infrastructure, and argue complex cases in court. But when it comes to money? Many freeze.

This isn't laziness or irresponsibility—it's neuroscience.

Neurological Roots: Fear Over Logic

Financial decision-making, especially investing, lights up some of the brain's most primal regions. Here's what fMRI scans show:

Brain Region	Response Trigger	Emotional Effect
Amygdala	Market volatility	Fear and anxiety
Anterior Insula	Potential loss scenarios	Disgust/avoidance
Prefrontal Cortex	Rational planning	Often overridden by emotion

The result? Even logical professionals default to their "lizard brain" when faced with money decisions. They avoid action

—not because they don't understand the numbers, but because those numbers trigger emotional discomfort.

The Ostrich Effect: Ignorance Feels Safer

It's called the "Ostrich Effect": the tendency to avoid financial information when we're stressed. A 2022 Fidelity study revealed that during market downturns, **login attempts dropped 41%**—people simply stopped checking their accounts.

But here's the kicker: those who *didn't look* actually performed **3.2x better annually**. Why? Because they weren't tempted to make impulsive decisions. They let time and compounding do the work.

Avoidance feels like failure, but sometimes it's accidental genius.

Takeaway: The System Isn't Designed for You

If you've been feeling overwhelmed, ashamed, or stuck—congratulations, you're human. The financial system wasn't built for clarity. It's an attention economy that thrives on confusion, urgency, and fear.

But now that you understand the psychological forces at play, you can begin to sidestep the trap. And the first step is realizing: *You don't need to be perfect. You just need a system.*

Section 2: Myth-Busting With Hard Data

Myth #1: "I'll Just Wait for the Right Time to Invest"

One of the most persistent myths in personal finance is the idea that successful investing is about timing the market—waiting for that "perfect" moment to buy in.

The data says otherwise.

A 20-year analysis (2003–2023) compared several strategies for a $10,000 investment. The results are staggering:

Strategy	$10,000 Becomes	Underperformance vs. Buy-and-Hold
Perfect Timing	$224,000	N/A (Theoretical Only)
Buy-and-Hold	$208,000	Baseline
Missed Top 10 Days	$104,000	-50%
Typical Market Timer	$67,000	-68%

You read that right: **Missing just the 10 best days in 20 years cuts your return in half**. And most market timers miss far more than that.

Why? Because fear-driven decisions almost always strike at the wrong time.

The Timing Trap: Behavioral Data from Real Investors

Dalbar, a research firm specializing in investor behavior, tracked 30 years of market flows and found that:

- **89% of "sell" decisions happen within 3 days of a market bottom**—when fear is highest.
- The average investor underperforms the market by **4.7% annually**, purely due to poor timing decisions.

In other words, it's not the market that fails us—it's our emotions. Waiting for a signal, a crash, a tip... it's all just another form of procrastination disguised as strategy.

Myth #2: "It's Too Late to Start Small"

Many beginners believe they've missed the boat if they're not investing thousands of dollars at a time. But small contributions grow faster than most people think, thanks to the magic of compound interest.

We'll dive deeper into this in the next section, but here's a teaser:

> Investing **just $5 a day** can grow into **over $228,000 in 30 years** at a 7% return.

That's a coffee a day—or a streaming subscription you won't miss.

The real myth isn't that timing works. It's that waiting will help you "get it right" later. In truth, waiting is the most expensive decision you can make.

The Bottom Line: You Can't Outguess the Market

If you're trying to time your way into wealth, stop. The people who try to outsmart the market usually outsmart only themselves. Instead, start building the habit of consistency. That's how real investors win—not with perfect guesses, but with predictable behaviors.

In the next section, we'll show how even the tiniest investments, done consistently, can snowball into life-changing wealth.

Section 3: The Compound Growth Imperative

The $5/Day Revolution

What if you could turn pocket change into a portfolio?

Thanks to the power of compound interest, you can. And you don't need to be a math wizard or a market guru—you just need time, consistency, and a little patience.

Let's break it down.

Daily Investment	After 10 Years	After 20 Years	After 30 Years
$5/day	$26,000	$87,000	$228,000
$10/day	$52,000	$174,000	$456,000
$25/day	$130,000	$435,000	$1.14 million

Assumes a 7% annual return (historical average for diversified equity portfolios)

The takeaway? **Small amounts, invested early and consistently, create massive results over time.** You don't need $10,000. You need five bucks and a recurring deposit button.

The Real-World Case: The Janitor Millionaire

One of the most famous examples of compound growth in action is Ronald Read, a janitor from Vermont who shocked the world in 2014 when he passed away leaving an **$8 million estate**.

His secret?

- He **invested $50/week** in dividend-paying blue-chip stocks.
- He **never sold.** He just reinvested.
- He **lived simply** and ignored financial hype.

No windfalls. No crypto. Just patience, habit, and time.

Ronald Read didn't need a financial advisor. He just needed to trust the math.

Why Compound Growth Works So Well

It's not about what you invest—it's about *when* and *for how long*.

Here's how the math works:

- In the early years, your returns are small—maybe $300 in growth in year one.
- But in year 20, your returns can add $10,000 or more *per year*—without doing anything differently.
- Eventually, **your money makes more than you do.**

That's the point where wealth becomes inevitable, not optional.

The Emotional Obstacle: "It Feels Too Slow"

Here's why most people never see the benefits of compounding: **it's boring at first**. It doesn't give you a dopamine hit. It's not flashy. But that's the point.

Compounding is the one get-rich-slow scheme that actually works.

Think of it like planting an oak tree. For years, it's just a twig. Then—suddenly—it's too big to ignore.

Bottom Line: The Earlier You Start, the Easier It Gets

If you're 25 and start investing $5 a day, you can hit $1 million by retirement. If you're 45? You'll need to invest 5x more to get there.

Time is your greatest asset. And the best moment to start was yesterday. The second best is today.

Section 4: The Information Toxicity Crisis

Why You're More Confused the More You Learn

In theory, more information should make you feel more confident. In practice? It often does the opposite.

In today's hyper-connected world, financial content is everywhere—YouTube channels, Reddit threads, TikTok influencers, endless blog posts and hot takes. It's a firehose of opinions, strategies, and contradictions. And for beginners, it leads to one thing:

Paralysis by analysis.

The Modern Investor's Diet (2023 Data)

According to a 2023 media consumption study, the average aspiring investor consumes:

- **11.7 finance articles per week**
- **6.3 hours of financial YouTube**
- **8.4 finance influencers across social platforms**

It's a full-time job just to *follow the noise*. But all this input doesn't result in better action. In fact, it has the opposite effect.

Cognitive Load: When More is Too Much

Studies in behavioral economics show that as decision complexity increases, decision quality *declines*. A Stanford study found:

- When given more than **3 options**, decision fatigue sets in rapidly.
- Each additional datapoint increases **anxiety by 17%** (MIT cognitive science lab).

So while the market moves at a steady pace, your brain starts spinning faster—and making worse choices.

The 3-Filter Solution: Curate, Don't Consume

To protect your mental bandwidth and improve financial decision-making, filter your information sources aggressively.

Filter 1: Source

Only follow **licensed fiduciaries** or professionals with at least a **10-year performance track record**. Avoid self-proclaimed "experts" with no credentials or verifiable results.

Filter 2: Frequency

Check updates **once a month**—not daily. Markets are noisy in the short term and wise over the long term. Let your brain breathe.

Filter 3: Format

Prefer **written analysis** over video or social media. Why?

- Written content reduces **emotional bias** by 37% (according to a 2022 University of Michigan study).
- It slows you down—so you actually *think*, instead of react.

The "Less is More" Investing Principle

The best investors aren't the ones with the most tabs open. They're the ones who can *filter out the noise* and focus on a clear, repeatable process.

Information isn't power—**discernment** is.

The good news? Once you reduce the input, your confidence skyrockets. Your focus sharpens. And your plan gets executed.

Up next, we'll look at one of the most powerful tools modern investors have—especially those starting small: **fractional shares and micro-investing**.

Section 5: The Micro-Investing Breakthrough

"I Don't Have Enough to Start" is Now a Myth

For decades, investing came with a gatekeeper: the minimum deposit.

- Want to buy a single Amazon share? That used to cost over $3,000.
- Vanguard funds? Many required $1,000 just to enter.
- The result? Millions of would-be investors assumed they weren't "ready."

But that barrier is gone.

Enter **fractional shares**—the single most underrated financial innovation for beginner investors in the last 20 years.

What Are Fractional Shares?

Fractional shares let you buy a **slice** of a stock or ETF instead of a full unit. Want to invest $10 in Apple, even if one share costs $180? You can. It's like buying 1/18 of a pizza slice—and it still tastes just as good over time.

Micro-investing platforms now let you start with as little as **$1**, making investing **as easy as rounding up your spare change.**

Platform Comparison (2023)

Broker	Minimum Investment	Offers Fractionals?	Auto-Invest Option?
Fidelity	$0	☑ Yes	☑ Yes
Schwab	$0	☑ Yes	✗ No
Vanguard	$1,000	✗ No	☑ Yes

The takeaway? Fidelity and Schwab are fully accessible to first-time investors with little to no capital. Vanguard remains better for larger, long-term investors.

Why This Matters: Behavior > Budget

A massive study of beginner investors on fractional-share platforms revealed:

- **Users saved 3.2x more consistently** than traditional brokerage users.
- **Portfolio balances grew 47% faster** on average—because small, frequent contributions beat sporadic big ones.

Why? Because it builds *identity*. When you invest—even $5—you stop being a bystander and start thinking like an owner. And that changes everything.

The Real Power of Micro-Investing: Momentum

This isn't about turning $5 into $5 million overnight.

It's about **getting in motion**. Starting a habit. Creating proof that you can do this.

When people start micro-investing, they're more likely to:

- Increase contributions within 60 days
- Check their balances less frequently
- Feel less intimidated by market volatility

It's a behavioral unlock. And for new investors, **behavior is the game**.

No More Excuses: Your Future Is for Sale—Cheap

You don't need thousands of dollars to begin.

You need a phone, an app, and a decision.

> Because the best investors aren't rich when they start— they're consistent.

Up next, we'll show how automation takes everything we've talked about so far—and turns it into a self-running system. It's time for **The Automated Wealth Machine**.

Section 6: The Automated Wealth Machine

Set It and Seriously Forget It

If you've ever said, *"I'll start investing once I have more time,"* this section is for you.

Life gets busy. Bills pile up. Motivation fades. But wealth-building doesn't have to rely on willpower. The most successful investors **remove themselves from the process entirely.**

Enter: **Automation.**

The Rise of Robo-Advisors

Robo-advisors are automated investment platforms that build, manage, and rebalance a diversified portfolio for you—based on your goals, risk tolerance, and timeline. You answer a few questions, and it does the heavy lifting.

Think of it as cruise control for your finances.

2023 Robo-Advisor Performance

Platform	5-Year Return	Compared to Human Advisor
Betterment	+9.1%	+0.7% better
Wealthfront	+8.9%	+0.5% better
Human Advisor (Avg)	+8.4%	Baseline

Not only are these platforms efficient—they're outperforming traditional advisors on average, all while charging a fraction of the fees.

Why Automation Works So Well

Let's break down what automating your investments actually does:

☑ **Eliminates Emotion**

- No more trying to "guess" when to buy or sell.
- No panic-selling during crashes.
- No FOMO-buying during hype cycles.

☑ **Builds Consistency**

- Set a recurring deposit ($10/week, $100/month—whatever works).
- It runs quietly in the background while you live your life.

☑ **Reinforces Smart Behavior**

- Automatically rebalances your portfolio to keep you aligned with your goals.
- Some even offer **tax-loss harvesting**, helping reduce your tax bill automatically.

The Psychology of Automation

Research shows that automating your money is more than a strategy—it's a mindset shift.

Users who automate report:

- **63% lower stress levels** about money
- **41% higher long-term savings rates**
- **89% less trading activity**, meaning fewer costly mistakes

Automation protects you from *you*—your fear, your distraction, your second-guessing.

> Because the best investment strategy is the one you don't have to think about.

Automation = Identity Shift

When you automate your investments, you stop being someone who's *trying* to build wealth. You become someone who already *is.*

It's not about hustle, or luck, or timing. It's about creating a system that runs whether you're motivated or not.

And the best part? You can set it up in an hour. And then never touch it again.

Next up, we'll dive into **The Anti-Panic Protocol**—a simple, science-backed response plan for when markets drop, headlines scream, and emotions spike.

Section 7: The Anti-Panic Protocol

Don't Just Do Something—Stand There

When markets crash, most people react the same way:

- **They freeze.**
- **They panic.**
- **They sell.**

That's not a character flaw—it's a brain feature. Your mind is hardwired to treat financial losses like physical danger.

But here's the truth: **almost every financial mistake is made in a moment of emotional turbulence.**

That's why you don't need a better prediction strategy—you need a **panic playbook**.

The 5-Minute Stabilization Method

This protocol is your emotional fire extinguisher. Use it *immediately* when the headlines scream "CRASH!" and you're tempted to bail.

🔄 Step 1: Physiological Reset

Before touching your portfolio, calm your nervous system.

- Use the **4-7-8 breathing technique**:
    - Breathe in for 4 seconds
    - Hold for 7 seconds
    - Breathe out for 8 seconds

Research from Mayo Clinic shows this reduces cortisol (stress hormone) by **39%** in under 5 minutes.

? Step 2: Perspective Reset

Zoom out. Market crashes are scary—but they're also **normal**. Look at the data:

- **Average bear market**: -33%, lasts 14 months
- **Average recovery**: Full rebound in 3.3 years
- **S&P 500**: Has recovered from *every single* crash in history

Selling in a panic guarantees losses. Staying the course has always recovered them.

🛠 Step 3: Action Protocol

Once you're calm, take these steps **only if necessary**:

✅ **Rebalance if allocations drift by more than 5%**

- Let's say your target is 80% stocks, 20% bonds.
- If stocks drop and you're now 70/30—buy more stocks to realign.

✅ **Consider tax-loss harvesting**

- If you're in a taxable account, selling losses can reduce your tax bill.

❌ **NEVER sell within 30 days of a drop**

- This is when mistakes happen. Set a 30-day rule: no panic trades.

The Hidden Advantage of Not Looking

During market dips, Fidelity found that login attempts dropped **41%**—and those accounts outperformed active traders by **3.2x annually**.

Why? Because they didn't flinch. They let the system ride.

> Sometimes, **doing nothing is the smartest financial move you can make.**

Your New Emergency Plan: Save It, Print It, Trust It

This Anti-Panic Protocol is not a feel-good trick—it's a behavioral defense mechanism.

Every major investor—Warren Buffett, Jack Bogle, Morgan Housel—has said the same thing in different words: **stay calm, stay invested.**

Now you don't have to wing it. You have a plan.

Next up, we'll bring it all home with **real-life case studies**—everyday people who built serious wealth by sticking to simple strategies.

Section 8: The Millionaire Next Door Playbook

Wealth Doesn't Always Drive a Tesla

The richest people you've never heard of often shop at Costco, wear beat-up sneakers, and check their net worth once a year. They don't chase stock tips, time the market, or live on CNBC.

They do three things really well:

1. **They save consistently.**
2. **They automate everything.**
3. **They leave it alone.**

Let's meet some of them.

📦 The UPS Driver With a $5 Million Portfolio

Who: A delivery driver in his 60s
Strategy:

- Maxed out his **401(k)** for over 30 years
- Participated in **Employee Stock Purchase Plan (ESPP)** every paycheck
- Invested in simple index funds

Secret Weapon:
He **never checked his balance more than once a year**.
He didn't try to outsmart the market—he just showed up, paycheck after paycheck.

📈 Result: A portfolio worth over **$5 million** by retirement.

🏫 The Teacher Couple With a $3.2M Net Worth

Who: Two public school teachers in the Midwest
Strategy:

- Every **raise** went straight into their **Vanguard auto-investing account**
- Lived on one salary, invested the other
- Used **municipal bonds** to reduce tax drag in taxable accounts

Their Philosophy:
Wealth isn't what you spend—**it's what you keep**.

💼 Result: A $3.2 million net worth by their late 50s, all while taking summers off.

The Janitor Millionaire (Yes, Really)

Who: Ronald Read, a Vermont janitor and gas station attendant
Strategy:

- Invested **$50/week** in blue-chip dividend-paying stocks
- Reinvested dividends for decades
- Lived incredibly frugally

When he died in 2014, his estate shocked everyone—including his family.

💰 Result: Left behind **$8 million**.

The Pattern: Slow, Boring, Unshakable

These people didn't:

- Chase hot stocks
- Panic during recessions
- Follow finance influencers

They did:

- Automate their savings
- Ignore the noise
- Play the long game

None of them had Wall Street jobs. None were born rich. They just **committed to a plan—and stuck with it.**

Your Takeaway: Copy the Boring People

You don't need to be flashy, brilliant, or lucky. You just need a simple, repeatable process.

> Wealth is a lagging indicator of consistency—not intelligence.

These stories aren't outliers. They're blueprints.

And now it's your turn. In the final section, we'll help you **build your own personalized plan** in just 7 days—no experience required.

Section 9: Your Personalized Start Plan

It's Time to Stop Consuming—and Start Building

By now, you've seen:

- Why so many smart people avoid investing
- How myths and misinformation keep beginners stuck
- The simple, data-backed strategies that quietly build wealth

You don't need more theory. You need *momentum*.

Here's your **7-Day Implementation Challenge**—designed to turn information into transformation.

📅 Day 1: Open Your Brokerage Account

Pick a platform with:

- No minimums
- Fractional shares
- Automatic investing

Best beginner choices (2024): Fidelity or Schwab
✅ Takes ~15 minutes
✅ You are now officially "an investor"

💸 Day 2: Set Up a $10 Recurring Investment

Pick a schedule: weekly or monthly
Choose a fund (ex: S&P 500 index, total market ETF)
Turn on automatic deposits

You now own assets that grow while you sleep.

📝 Day 3: Write Your Investment Policy Statement

This is your **"emotional firewall"**. It should include:

- Your long-term goal (e.g. retirement at 60, buy a home in 10 years)
- Your risk tolerance (e.g. "I can handle a 30% drop without selling")
- Your rules (e.g. "Never sell within 30 days of a downturn")

Keep it simple—one page max.

🚫 Day 4: Block the Noise

Install browser extensions or phone apps that:

- Block finance sites you compulsively check
- Limit social media exposure to market "experts"

More data = more anxiety. Set boundaries.

📅 Day 5: Schedule Your Annual Review

Put it in your calendar now. Once per year:

- Check portfolio balance
- Rebalance if needed
- Increase contributions if possible

You're building a system, not micromanaging it.

🤝 Day 6: Share Your Plan

Find an accountability partner:

- A friend, spouse, coworker, or online community
- Share your goals and your policy statement
- Ask them to check in with you in 3 months

Behavior sticks better when it's visible.

🎉 Day 7: Celebrate Your First Investment

Yes, even if it's just $5.

Take a photo. Journal it. Post it (if that's your style). You just crossed the starting line most people *never* reach.

That first step? It's not small—it's everything.

Final Words: You're Not Late. You're Early.

The beginner's trap is built on myths:

- "You need a lot of money to start."
- "The market is too risky right now."
- "I'll invest when I feel ready."

The truth?

Starting small, starting now, and sticking with it beats everything else.

You now have the mindset, the tools, the plan—and the evidence that it works. Whether your goal is $100,000 or $10 million, the journey starts the same way:

> With one account.
> One automatic deposit.
> And one decision to not quit.

The Truth About Investing for Beginners — What No One Tells You

So you're thinking about investing — great move. But here's the problem: beginner investors are bombarded with the same generic advice over and over again. "Start early," "diversify," "don't time the market." While all of that *technically* holds up, it barely scratches the surface of what actually matters when you're just starting out.

Let's flip the script. Here's what most people get **dead wrong** about investing — and what you *actually* need to know before you dive in.

💸 Myth #1: You Need Thousands to Start Investing

Truth: You can start with as little as $5.
Apps like Robinhood, Acorns, and M1 Finance let you buy **fractional shares**, meaning you can invest in companies like Apple or Google without needing hundreds of dollars. The

key isn't *how much* you invest — it's *how consistently* you invest.

> 💡 **Pro Tip:** Set up automatic transfers, even if it's just $10 a week. Build the habit first — the wealth comes later.

💰 Myth #2: Investing Is Riskier Than Saving

Truth: Not investing is actually riskier in the long run. Inflation eats away at your savings every year. If your savings account is paying 1% interest and inflation is 3%, you're *losing money* while it sits.

> ⚠ **Pitfall:** Don't over-save. Once your emergency fund is covered (3-6 months of expenses), start putting your money to work through investing.

🕒 Myth #3: You Should Wait for the "Right Time"

Truth: The best time to start investing was yesterday. The second-best time? Today.
Trying to time the market is a fool's game — even pros can't do it consistently. What actually works? **Time in the market**, not timing the market.

> 💡 **Pro Tip:** Use **dollar-cost averaging** — invest a fixed amount at regular intervals. It smooths out the highs and lows and builds discipline.

📉 Myth #4: Bonds Are Boring and Useless

Truth: Bonds are the calm in the storm.
Young investors often overlook bonds thinking they're just for retirees. But bonds reduce portfolio volatility and provide income even during market downturns.

> 💡 **Pro Tip:** Consider a **target-date fund** — it automatically adjusts your mix of stocks and bonds based on your age.

🤖 Myth #5: Robo-Advisors Handle *Everything*

Truth: Robo-advisors are helpful but not perfect.
They're great for hands-off investing, but you still need to understand your goals, fees, and risk tolerance.

> ⚠ **Pitfall:** Don't assume your portfolio is optimized. Check in at least once a year to make sure it's aligned with your current life goals.

📊 Myth #6: "Safe" Stocks Can't Drop

Truth: Every stock carries risk — even the big names.
Just because a company is famous doesn't mean it's invincible (hello, 2008 financial crisis).

> 💡 **Pro Tip:** Don't fall in love with brand names. Focus on **diversification** and invest in **index funds or ETFs** that spread your risk across hundreds of companies.

💸 Myth #7: Fees Don't Matter If You're Making Money

Truth: Fees are wealth killers.
That 1% annual fee might not sound like much, but over 30 years, it can eat up *over 25%* of your potential earnings.

> 💡 **Pro Tip:** Look for funds with **expense ratios below 0.10%** and avoid actively managed mutual funds with high hidden costs.

▯ Myth #8: Taxes Only Matter When You Sell

Truth: The IRS loves your dividends, interest, and gains — even if you reinvest them.
Most beginners forget about the tax implications of investing, especially in **taxable accounts**.

> 💡 **Pro Tip:** Start with **tax-advantaged accounts** like Roth IRAs or 401(k)s to grow your money tax-free or tax-deferred.

> ⚠ **Pitfall:** Selling investments you've held for less than a year? You'll pay *short-term capital gains tax* — which is usually higher than long-term.

Final Thoughts

The world of investing can feel intimidating, especially when you're hit with conflicting advice and outdated rules. But when you start peeling back the layers, you'll see that smart investing isn't about luck or timing — it's about clarity, consistency, and cutting through the noise.

Start small. Learn fast. And remember: your future self is already grateful you began.

Chapter 2

How to Stop Panicking (Even When CNBC Screams "CRASH!")

In the fast-paced world of investing, it's easy to fall prey to panic when financial markets take a sharp downturn. The headlines scream "Market Crash!" and financial news outlets, like CNBC, keep blaring warnings of impending doom. The natural response? Anxiety. Fear. The urge to take immediate action. But here's the key takeaway: while volatility is uncomfortable, it's not inherently dangerous. In fact, the very nature of the stock market requires you to stay calm and think long-term, rather than succumb to fear in the face of temporary fluctuations.

Why Volatility Feels Scary (But Isn't Dangerous)

Market volatility often triggers emotional reactions because it taps into our deep-seated psychological instincts. Humans are hardwired to respond to uncertainty and risk. In prehistoric times, quick reactions to potential threats were critical for survival. Today, however, our survival instincts manifest when the stock market drops, making us want to act quickly—often irrationally. The emotional response we have to market swings is disproportionate to the actual risks involved, and that's where the danger lies.

The reality, however, is far less scary than the headlines make it out to be. Over the last several decades, the S&P 500

—often used as a benchmark for the broader market—has experienced a 10% or greater drop every single year since 1980. Yet, despite these routine drops, the average annual return for the S&P 500 during this time has been a healthy 10%. Think about that for a second: even though the market frequently experiences significant declines, it has consistently recovered and delivered strong long-term returns.

This demonstrates an important concept: while market dips feel intense in the moment, they are usually short-lived and often followed by periods of growth. Take a look at some of the most dramatic drops in history, such as the 2008 financial crisis or the 2020 market crash triggered by the COVID-19 pandemic. Both events caused major disruptions, yet both were followed by rapid and robust recoveries. The volatility, though unsettling, is not as dangerous as it appears when you look at the long-term trends.

The Panic-Proof Checklist: A Step-by-Step Guide to Staying Calm

When the headlines are filled with ominous warnings of a "market meltdown," how can you avoid making rash decisions? Here's a simple, proven checklist to follow when you feel the urge to panic:

1. **Turn off alerts.**
   Constantly checking your phone for updates on the stock market can heighten anxiety. Alerts, notifications,

and social media posts about the latest drop can create unnecessary stress. If you need to, mute alerts or delete financial apps from your phone temporarily. This gives you the breathing room you need to think clearly without being overwhelmed by sensationalist news.

2. **Re-read your "Why" statement.**
   In Chapter 3, you will write a personal "Why" statement—this is your core reason for investing. Whether you're saving for retirement, building wealth for future generations, or funding a child's education, your "Why" is your guiding star. During moments of market volatility, revisit this statement. It will remind you of the bigger picture and refocus your mindset on your long-term goals. When you understand your purpose for investing, short-term market drops become less significant.

3. **Consult your "Bear Market Playbook."**
   A key part of investing is having a plan for when things go wrong. You should already have a playbook in place —written down and easy to access—that guides your actions during bear markets. Flip to Chapter 7 to review your strategy during downturns. Whether it's adjusting your portfolio, taking advantage of buying opportunities, or sticking to your investment philosophy, following your pre-determined strategy is

one of the best ways to stay grounded during turbulent times.

The "Paper Hands" Test: Are You Ready for the Storm?

One of the most revealing tests of an investor's risk tolerance is imagining a significant drop in their portfolio's value. Let's say your portfolio suddenly drops by 30% tomorrow. How would you feel? Would you be ready to sell your investments to "cut your losses," or would you stick to your long-term strategy?

If your immediate reaction is to sell, it's likely a sign that you're taking on too much risk relative to your comfort level. No one likes seeing their hard-earned money drop in value, but if you panic in the face of volatility, it suggests that your portfolio may not be well-aligned with your personal risk tolerance. A well-constructed portfolio should give you the confidence to weather market storms without overreacting.

To fix this, consider adjusting the balance of stocks and bonds in your portfolio. If the thought of a 30% drop triggers a sell-off response, your asset allocation may be too aggressive for your risk tolerance. Shift toward a more conservative mix of assets to help you feel comfortable with fluctuations in the market. The goal is to create a portfolio that helps you stay calm even when the market is turbulent.

Understanding Risk: The Key to Long-Term Success

At the core of every financial strategy is the concept of risk. Risk is a natural part of investing, but managing it is essential for long-term success. In times of market volatility, it's crucial to remember that risk is not the same as danger. Risk is simply the possibility of loss; danger arises when we make hasty, emotion-driven decisions that jeopardize our financial goals.

Building a resilient mindset starts with understanding the risks you are taking and ensuring that your portfolio matches your risk tolerance. If you understand the risks involved and have a clear strategy for managing them, you'll be less likely to panic when the market turns south. This approach will help you remain calm, composed, and focused on your ultimate financial objectives.

Riding the Waves of Volatility

The financial markets will inevitably experience ups and downs. Volatility is not only unavoidable but also essential for long-term growth. The key is to manage your emotions and stay focused on your long-term goals. By following the Panic-Proof Checklist, revisiting your "Why" statement, and ensuring that your portfolio aligns with your risk tolerance, you can remain calm in the face of market fluctuations.

Remember, market crashes are temporary. The resilience of the markets over time is proof that volatility doesn't spell the end—it's simply part of the journey. With the right mindset and strategy, you can avoid the panic and stay on course toward financial success. The market may ebb and flow, but your long-term plan can keep you grounded, even in turbulent times.

The Trust Crisis – How to Spot BS Advice

In the world of investing, trust is paramount. Unfortunately, in a landscape filled with high-stakes financial decisions, it's also one of the easiest things to lose. Scams, misleading information, and "guru" advice run rampant across the internet, social media, and even traditional media channels. As a novice investor or even a seasoned one, it's essential to navigate this sea of noise and spot the red flags of bad advice. After all, a single misstep could derail years of financial progress.

In this chapter, we'll dive deep into how to recognize bad financial advice, how to ask the right questions before taking advice, and what to do when you find yourself unsure about the credibility of your financial sources. Understanding how to spot and avoid scams and high-risk investment strategies is critical to safeguarding your financial future.

Red Flags of Gurus and Scams

It's easy to get drawn into the allure of financial gurus and so-called experts who promise to make you rich. They often present themselves as having insider knowledge or a "secret formula" for success. But here's the harsh truth: **there's no such thing as a guaranteed return**, and if something sounds too good to be true, it probably is. Here are the top red flags to watch out for when evaluating investment advice:

⚐ "Guaranteed Returns" – No Such Thing

One of the most common (and dangerous) promises you'll encounter is the claim of "guaranteed returns." Whether it's through social media ads, email newsletters, or even televised commercials, these promises sound enticing: "Invest today and make 20% returns every year!"

The truth is simple: **there is no such thing as a guaranteed return.** If it were that easy, everyone would be a millionaire. The markets are inherently unpredictable. Investments—whether in stocks, bonds, real estate, or anything else—carry risk, and that risk can't be avoided. Anyone promising guaranteed returns is likely either uninformed or attempting to deceive you.

Even so-called "safe" investments like bonds or CDs come with their own set of risks, including inflation risk, interest rate risk, and others. If a financial advisor or guru promises guaranteed returns, it's a significant red flag, and you should immediately be skeptical.

⚐ "Secret Strategy" – If It Worked, Why Sell It?

Another common red flag is the promise of a "secret strategy" that will make you rich. Whether it's a trading system, a stock-picking method, or some obscure investment technique, these offers sound tempting. After all, who doesn't want to get in on a "secret" that guarantees massive wealth?

However, the key question to ask is: **If this strategy is so effective, why is it being sold?** If someone had a true secret strategy that could consistently beat the market or generate outsized returns, they wouldn't be selling it—they would be using it themselves. The very fact that they're marketing it to others suggests it's not the magic bullet they claim it to be.

Strategies like these are often packaged in complex language and high-pressure sales pitches to get you to act quickly. Don't fall for the illusion. If you're hearing the words "exclusive," "secret," or "insider knowledge," take a step back and ask yourself if this person has your best interests in mind.

⚐ Pressure to Act NOW – Fear Sells

There's one tactic that all financial scams have in common: urgency. "Act now!" "This opportunity won't last!" "The market is about to skyrocket, and you don't want to miss out!" If you hear these phrases, especially when it's tied to an offer or a product, it's time to be cautious.

Fear is a powerful motivator, and many marketers and scammers use it to prompt quick decisions. But investing is not about immediate gratification—it's about making well-reasoned decisions that align with your long-term goals. You should never feel pressured to make a decision quickly when it comes to investing. Good investments require thoughtful research, planning, and time. Any strategy that's pushing you to act in haste is likely not in your best interest.

The Fiduciary Test: Protect Yourself Before Taking Advice

So, how can you separate the trustworthy advisors from the sharks in the water? Start by asking the right questions. The answers to these questions will give you insight into whether or not the person you're dealing with has your best interests at heart.

1. Are you a fiduciary?

A fiduciary is someone who is legally obligated to act in your best interest, above their own. If an advisor is a fiduciary, they must prioritize your needs and provide advice that's best for you—even if it means they earn less money or have to recommend something less profitable for themselves. This is a critical distinction.

However, not all financial advisors are fiduciaries. Some are only required to act in a "suitability" standard, meaning that they only need to recommend products that are appropriate for you, not necessarily the best. **Before taking advice, always ask if the person is a fiduciary.** If they say no, proceed with caution.

2. How do you get paid?

Understanding how an advisor is compensated is crucial. There are two main types of payment structures for financial advisors: commission-based and fee-only.

- **Commission-based advisors** make money by selling specific financial products (e.g., insurance policies, annuities, mutual funds). While this structure isn't inherently bad, it can introduce conflicts of interest. A commission-based advisor might be more inclined to sell products that pay them more in commissions, rather than the best product for you.
- **Fee-only advisors** are compensated solely through flat fees or hourly charges for their services. They don't receive commissions for selling products, so their advice is likely more objective and unbiased. **Fee-only advisors** are often a better choice, as they're not incentivized to sell you anything other than what's best for you.

3. Can you show me your long-term track record?

No reputable financial advisor or guru should expect you to take their advice without showing some evidence of their success. Ask to see their long-term track record, not just their best returns or their "hottest tips." A credible advisor will be able to provide you with historical data and references, showing how their strategies have performed over the long run.

Avoid getting swept up in hype or "one-off" success stories. Anyone can point to a great trade or a short-term gain, but it's the long-term performance that matters. If an advisor or guru is hesitant to share their long-term track record, it's a sign that they might not have the experience or success they claim.

Safe Havens for Skeptics: Low-Risk Investment Options

For those who are understandably skeptical about high-risk advice and untrustworthy gurus, there are safe havens that provide stability without relying on market speculation or "secrets." These options are tried and tested, and while they might not offer the rapid returns that some are looking for, they are reliable ways to build wealth over time.

1. Index Funds – Own the Whole Market

Index funds are one of the best-kept secrets in investing. These funds track the performance of entire markets or sectors, such as the S&P 500 or the total U.S. stock market. By investing in an index fund, you're essentially owning a tiny portion of hundreds or thousands of companies, providing broad diversification without the need to pick individual stocks. One popular example is the **VTI** (Vanguard Total Stock Market ETF).

The beauty of index funds is their simplicity. They don't require constant monitoring or the need for "insider knowledge." Instead, they provide exposure to the overall growth of the economy. Over time, they generally outperform most actively managed funds, especially when factoring in their low fees.

2. Bonds – The "Training Wheels" of Investing

Bonds are often considered the "training wheels" of investing. While they typically offer lower returns than stocks, they are much less volatile and provide a reliable stream of income. Bonds are essentially loans you make to companies or governments, and they pay you interest in exchange for your investment.

Bonds are ideal for those looking for stability in their portfolio, particularly as they near retirement or want to balance risk with steady returns. They can also serve as a counterweight to the volatility of stocks.

3. Robo-Advisors – Low-Cost, Hands-Off Investing

Robo-advisors are automated platforms that create and manage a diversified portfolio for you based on your risk tolerance, goals, and preferences. They are a great option for hands-off investors who want to avoid picking stocks themselves but still want their money working for them. Many robo-advisors use low-cost index funds to build your portfolio.

While robo-advisors are a great option for beginners, it's important to be aware of their fees. While many of them are low-cost, some charge management fees that can eat into your returns over time. Be sure to understand all costs involved before choosing a robo-advisor.

Building Trust and Protecting Yourself

In a world filled with misleading advice and financial scams, it's essential to develop a keen sense of discernment. The ability to spot bad advice and steer clear of harmful strategies will safeguard your financial future. Remember the red flags to watch for: guaranteed returns, secret strategies, and high-pressure sales tactics. When in doubt, ask the right questions—**Are you a fiduciary? How do you get paid? Can you show me your long-term track record?**

Additionally, for those looking to stay on the safer side, consider low-risk, time-tested investment options like index funds, bonds, and robo-advisors. These tools will help you build wealth over time without falling victim to high-risk schemes or scams. Always remember that investing is a marathon, not a sprint—and building wealth takes patience, discipline, and the ability to discern trustworthy advice from the noise.

Chapter 3

The 1-Hour Starter Portfolio: Literally What to Do

Investing for the future can seem overwhelming, especially if you're just getting started. The financial world is full of jargon, complex strategies, and complicated products that can easily leave beginners feeling lost. But here's the good news: You don't need to spend years learning the ins and outs of investing to build a solid foundation. In fact, with just one hour of your time, you can create a simple, well-diversified portfolio that sets you on the path toward financial success.

This article will take you through the exact steps to build your **1-Hour Starter Portfolio**—a portfolio designed to give you broad market exposure with minimal effort, using only three carefully selected funds. Whether you're just starting out or looking for a low-maintenance investment strategy, this approach is perfect for those who want to get started without stress or confusion.

Step 1: Open an Investment Account

Before you can start investing, you need a brokerage account. This is where your investments will be held. Fortunately, setting up an investment account is easier than ever. Some of the best options for beginners are well-established, low-cost brokers like **Fidelity**, **Vanguard**, and **Charles Schwab**. These brokers are known for their user-friendly platforms, great customer support, and, most importantly, low fees.

Here's a breakdown of what to do:

1. **Choose a Broker:** Fidelity, Vanguard, or Schwab are excellent options for long-term investing, as they offer low fees, broad investment options, and educational resources for beginners. You can't go wrong with any of these choices.
2. **Complete the Application:** The application process is straightforward. You'll need to provide some personal information, such as your name, address, Social Security number, and employment details. The entire process can be done online, and most accounts are approved within a few minutes to a few days.
3. **Verify Your Identity:** For security purposes, you may need to provide additional documents to verify your identity. This could include uploading a copy of your driver's license or other official documents.
4. **Fund Your Account:** Once your account is approved, you'll be asked to deposit funds into your account. It doesn't matter if it's $50, $500, or $1,000—what's important is getting the ball rolling. Start with any amount that feels comfortable, and remember that you can always deposit more later.

Step 2: Deposit Any Amount (It Doesn't Matter)

A common misconception is that you need a large sum of money to start investing. This is simply not true. **The best time to start investing is today**, no matter how small your deposit is.

While many people think they need thousands of dollars to build a meaningful portfolio, the truth is that even modest contributions can compound over time, especially when invested wisely.

So, how much should you deposit? The answer: It doesn't matter.

Start with what you're comfortable with. You might decide to invest:

- $50 (to get started with a small but steady approach)
- $500 (to build a slightly more diversified foundation)
- $1,000 or more (to give your portfolio a strong initial boost)

The key is to start. Once you've made your first deposit, you'll be able to invest in a diversified set of funds that can work hard for you. And don't worry if you don't have a lot of money to start—what matters is the habit of investing regularly.

Step 3: Buy These 3 Funds

Now comes the exciting part: **choosing your investments**. You don't need to be an expert to select the right mix of assets. For most people, the goal is to create a portfolio that provides broad exposure to the market while minimizing the risk of large losses. The following three funds are a simple yet effective way to do just that:

1. **VTI – U.S. Stocks (60% of your portfolio)**
   VTI is the **Vanguard Total Stock Market ETF**, and it's an excellent choice for U.S. stock exposure. This fund includes a broad selection of U.S. companies, covering everything from large-cap blue chips to small-cap growth stocks. By investing in VTI, you're essentially buying the entire U.S. stock market, which means you get diversified exposure to the U.S. economy.

   Why 60%?
   A 60% allocation to stocks is a good balance between risk and reward. U.S. stocks have historically offered solid returns over the long term, and this fund provides exposure to the entire market, not just the largest companies. This diversification helps spread risk and gives you the potential for growth.

2. **BND – U.S. Bonds (30% of your portfolio)**
   BND is the **Vanguard Total Bond Market ETF**, which invests in a wide variety of U.S. government and corporate bonds. Bonds are typically less volatile than stocks and provide a more stable income stream.

Why 30%?
A 30% bond allocation is a great way to add stability to your portfolio. Bonds tend to perform better during economic downturns, helping to cushion the blow when stock markets fall. The goal here is to reduce overall volatility and protect your investments from wild swings. With 30% in bonds, you strike a healthy balance between growth and safety.

3. **VXUS – International Stocks (10% of your portfolio)**
VXUS is the **Vanguard Total International Stock ETF**, which invests in stocks from around the world, excluding the U.S. This fund provides exposure to developed and emerging markets across Europe, Asia, and beyond.

Why 10%?
While the U.S. market is the largest and most developed, it's also wise to diversify globally. Allocating a smaller portion (10%) to international stocks helps you tap into growth opportunities outside the U.S. It reduces your exposure to any one country's economic conditions and gives you a broader view of the global economy.

Step 4: Set Up Auto-Investing

One of the most powerful tools you can use to grow your investments is **auto-investing**. By setting up an automatic deposit into your investment account, you can make consistent contributions without having to think about it. Whether you invest $25 a week or $200 a month, the key is to make it automatic and routine.

Why Auto-Investing Works:

1. **Dollar-Cost Averaging:** By investing regularly, you buy more shares when prices are low and fewer shares when prices are high. Over time, this evens out the purchase price, reducing the impact of market volatility.
2. **Habit Formation:** Automating your investments means you're more likely to stick to your plan. Investing becomes a regular habit, which helps you avoid the temptation to time the market or make emotional decisions based on short-term market movements.
3. **Compounding Growth:** The more regularly you invest, the more you benefit from compounding. Your returns earn returns, which can significantly accelerate the growth of your portfolio over time.

Setting up auto-investing is easy. Once your account is funded, go to the auto-investment section on your brokerage platform (Fidelity, Vanguard, Schwab, etc.). You can choose to invest on a weekly, bi-weekly, or monthly basis—whatever works best for you. Even a small amount, such as $25 per week, can make a significant impact over time.

Step 5: Script for Your Future Self

Investing isn't just about numbers and returns—it's also about psychology. The market will experience ups and downs, and it's easy to get discouraged or tempted to sell when things get tough. That's why it's helpful to write a letter to your future self, reminding you of your long-term goals and reinforcing your commitment to stay the course.

Here's a sample script for your future self:

Dear [Your Name],

If you're reading this, the market probably dropped. Don't sell. This is normal.

Remember: You're investing for [your goal]. Whether it's saving for retirement, building wealth for your family, or funding a future project, you've already made the decision to invest for the long term. Market fluctuations are a natural part of the process. They happen every year, and they don't change your ultimate goal.

Check back in a year. If you've stayed invested, you'll likely see that the market has bounced back, and your portfolio is on track to grow. Don't let short-term noise derail your long-term success.

You've got this.

— Past You

By writing this letter, you create a touchstone that you can revisit during moments of doubt. It helps you stay focused on your long-term objectives, even when the market feels unpredictable or volatile.

Step 6: Monitor, But Don't Obsess

After setting up your 1-Hour Starter Portfolio, your job isn't over—but it's also not time to obsess over daily market fluctuations. Check in on your portfolio periodically, but resist the urge to make changes unless you have a significant life event (like a career change, marriage, or a change in financial goals). Regularly contributing to your portfolio and staying disciplined will serve you better than making frequent adjustments.

Starting is the Hardest Part

The first step in investing is often the hardest, but once you've completed your 1-Hour Starter Portfolio, you'll be set up for success. You'll have a diversified, low-cost portfolio that's designed to grow over time. More importantly, you'll have taken control of your financial future, which is the most important step toward building wealth.

So, don't wait. Take one hour today, set up your account, choose your funds, and get started. Your future self will thank you.

Chapter 4

The "Buckets" System – Never Fear a Crash Again

Investing can be an emotional rollercoaster. The stock market's volatility, economic downturns, and sudden crashes often cause investors to panic and make irrational decisions. As a result, many people either bail out of the market at the wrong time or, conversely, throw caution to the wind and invest in high-risk ventures without considering their long-term goals. But there's a way to invest that balances risk with peace of mind—the **Buckets System**.

The **Buckets System** is a simple yet powerful strategy that allows you to invest in a way that shields you from the emotional turmoil of market crashes, provides room for growth, and satisfies the need for some speculative fun—all without risking your entire financial future. By dividing your portfolio into three distinct "buckets," you can manage risk, ensure steady growth, and still indulge your stock-picking urges without jeopardizing your long-term objectives.

In this article, we will explore the **Buckets System** in detail, break down each of the three buckets, and explain why this method works. By the end, you'll have a clear roadmap for how to allocate your investments in a way that helps you sleep soundly at night—no matter what happens in the markets.

What is the Buckets System?

At its core, the **Buckets System** divides your investment portfolio into three separate "buckets," each with a different purpose and level of risk. These buckets are designed to protect you from the volatility of the market while still allowing you to grow your wealth over time.

1. **Bucket 1: "Never Touch" (40%)**
   This bucket is for your safe, low-risk investments—essentially, the money you won't need for many years. The goal of Bucket 1 is to provide peace of mind, knowing that you have a cushion of funds that can weather any market downturn.
2. **Bucket 2: "Growth Engine" (50%)**
   This bucket is designed for growth and is the backbone of your wealth-building strategy. It's allocated to investments like index funds, which provide long-term growth without excessive risk. This is your autopilot mode for growing your portfolio over time.
3. **Bucket 3: "Mad Money" (10%)**
   Bucket 3 is where you can indulge your urges to pick individual stocks or take on more risk. This is your opportunity to "play" in the market without jeopardizing your financial stability. Think of it as the portion of your portfolio where you take calculated risks for potential higher returns.

How to Split Your Money: The Three Buckets Explained

Bucket 1: "Never Touch" (40%)

This is the foundation of the **Buckets System**. Bucket 1 is designed to protect your money, offering safety and security in the face of market volatility. It consists of low-risk, stable investments that you can rely on when the market crashes. The primary goal of this bucket is to provide you with enough liquidity to cover your immediate needs without touching your riskier investments.

What Goes in Bucket 1?

- **Bonds:** Bonds are loans to companies or governments that pay interest over time. They are less volatile than stocks, making them a good choice for safe, steady returns. For example, U.S. Treasury bonds are considered some of the safest investments in the world.
- **Certificates of Deposit (CDs):** A CD is a low-risk investment where you deposit money with a bank for a fixed period in exchange for a guaranteed interest rate. They are ideal for people who want to preserve capital without worrying about market swings.
- **Cash and Cash Equivalents:** Cash, savings accounts, or money market funds also fall into this category. Having liquid assets ensures you have easy access to money when needed, without having to sell investments during market downturns.

Why 40%?

The **40% allocation** in Bucket 1 ensures that you have enough funds to cover your living expenses and financial obligations for several years. If the market crashes, Bucket 1 provides you with the necessary liquidity and stability to avoid selling investments during a downturn. This cushion also gives you time to let the market recover without feeling the immediate need to sell stocks or riskier investments.

In essence, Bucket 1 is your **sleep-at-night** money. When the market drops, you can rest easy knowing that your essential needs are covered and your long-term investments are not being compromised.

Bucket 2: "Growth Engine" (50%)

Bucket 2 is the engine that drives long-term growth in your portfolio. This portion of your money is allocated to investments that offer the potential for higher returns but still maintain a reasonable level of risk. These investments are for the future—your retirement, your children's education, or other long-term financial goals. The goal of this bucket is to grow your wealth over time, typically through broad-based market exposure.

What Goes in Bucket 2?

- **Index Funds:** Index funds, like **VTI (Vanguard Total Stock Market ETF)** and **VXUS (Vanguard Total International Stock ETF)**, are the backbone of this bucket. Index funds allow you to invest in a wide variety of stocks without having to pick individual companies. They provide broad market exposure, diversification, and low fees.

    - **VTI** covers the entire U.S. stock market, from large-cap companies to small-cap stocks.
    - **VXUS** provides exposure to international markets, ensuring that your portfolio isn't overly reliant on U.S. stocks.

- **ETFs (Exchange-Traded Funds):** ETFs are another great option for this bucket, as they allow you to invest in a diversified portfolio of stocks or bonds while maintaining a relatively low cost. ETFs trade like individual stocks, but they provide the benefits of diversification.

Why 50%?

A **50% allocation** to growth assets like index funds ensures that you're taking advantage of the long-term growth potential of the stock market without exposing yourself to the extreme risk of picking individual stocks. Index funds are designed to track the overall market, meaning they typically provide steady growth with lower volatility than stock-picking strategies.

Additionally, investing in both U.S. and international markets allows you to benefit from growth across different economies. By maintaining a **50% allocation**, you're positioning your portfolio for growth while still balancing the risks in Bucket 1.

Bucket 3: "Mad Money" (10%)

This bucket is where you get to have a little fun. Many investors feel the need to pick individual stocks or make speculative investments to try and maximize returns. Bucket 3 allows you to scratch that itch without compromising your long-term financial goals. The key to this bucket is that it is limited—**no more than 10%** of your total portfolio should be allocated here.

What Goes in Bucket 3?

- **Individual Stocks:** If you enjoy researching and picking stocks, Bucket 3 is your playground. You can pick individual stocks based on your research, whether it's for short-term speculation or long-term investment.
- **Cryptocurrency:** For the more adventurous investor, you might choose to allocate a small portion of this bucket to alternative investments like cryptocurrency. While volatile, cryptocurrencies have attracted attention for their potential for high returns.

Why 10%?

The **10% allocation** in Bucket 3 ensures that you can enjoy the thrill of stock picking or high-risk investments without putting your financial security at risk. If your investments in this bucket perform poorly, they won't significantly affect your overall financial situation. However, if they outperform, you'll get the satisfaction of knowing that you took calculated risks while protecting the bulk of your portfolio with Buckets 1 and 2.

This bucket satisfies your "Fear of Missing Out" (FOMO) urges without jeopardizing your future. If you see a hot stock or a new investment trend, you can indulge in it here—but always remember that it's a small portion of your portfolio.

Why This System Works:

The beauty of the **Buckets System** is that it offers a structured, low-stress approach to investing that takes into account both psychological and financial factors. Here's why this approach works:

1. Crashes? Bucket 1 Covers You.

Market crashes are inevitable. They happen regularly, and while the market eventually recovers, you don't want to be forced to sell investments at a loss during a downturn. Bucket 1 gives you the **peace of mind** to weather the storm. It provides you with safe, liquid assets that can cover your living expenses and other financial obligations without dipping into your riskier investments. When the market rebounds, you can take advantage of the recovery without having to make emotional decisions.

2. FOMO? Bucket 3 Lets You "Play" Without Risking Everything.

It's easy to get caught up in the excitement of the next big stock or investment trend. But the fear of missing out (FOMO) can lead to poor decision-making if you're too invested in high-risk assets. Bucket 3 provides you with the opportunity to indulge your stock-picking urges and invest in high-risk, high-reward opportunities—without putting your long-term financial goals in jeopardy. With just **10% of your portfolio** in play, you can take calculated risks without worrying about losing everything.

3. Simplicity and Structure.

The Buckets System is straightforward and easy to implement. With clear guidelines for how to split your assets into three categories, you eliminate the stress of trying to constantly monitor and adjust your portfolio. The system works with minimal effort, and you can rest easy knowing your portfolio is balanced between safety, growth, and a little fun.

Take Control of Your Future with the Buckets System

The **Buckets System** is a simple yet powerful strategy that can help you navigate the complexities of investing while ensuring that you can weather any market downturn. By dividing your portfolio into three distinct buckets, you can build wealth steadily while maintaining peace of mind.

- **Bucket 1** ensures that your immediate needs are covered with low-risk investments that provide stability.
- **Bucket 2** powers long-term growth through diversified index funds and ETFs, with a focus on low-cost, broad market exposure.
- **Bucket 3** allows you to indulge in individual stocks or more speculative investments, knowing that it's just a small part of your overall strategy.

This approach reduces the emotional toll of investing, helps you stay focused on your long-term goals, and ensures that you never have to fear a crash again. By following the **Buckets System**, you'll have the confidence to invest wisely and protect your financial future—no matter what the markets throw your way.

Chapter 5

Bonds for Beginners (The Secret Safety Net)

Why Bonds = Training Wheels for New Investors

The Unsung Hero of Investing

Imagine you're learning to ride a bike. Stocks are the thrill of coasting downhill—fast, exhilarating, but prone to wipeouts. Bonds? They're the training wheels. Not flashy, but they keep you upright when the road gets rocky.

Most people jump into investing with dreams of stock market glory. But the truth is, the *real* pros always keep a safety net—and that net is bonds. For beginner investors, bonds can provide steady income, lower volatility, and a sense of control when the market spins like a carnival ride.

This guide is your go-to breakdown of bonds: what they are, why they matter, how to buy them (without falling into jargon traps), and the underrated "ladder trick" that makes them work like clockwork.

What the Heck is a Bond, Really?

Let's cut the Wall Street buzzwords and get to the point.

A Bond = A Loan You Give

When you buy a bond, you're lending money to a company or government. In return, they promise to pay you back—plus a little extra called **interest**.

Simple, right?

You can think of it like this:

- **Stocks** = You're buying a piece of the business (ownership).
- **Bonds** = You're lending money to the business or government (debt).

Why Do People Buy Bonds?

Three core reasons:

1. **Steady Income**: Bonds pay you interest, usually every 6 months.
2. **Lower Risk**: Unlike stocks, bonds tend to hold up better in bad markets.
3. **Diversification**: They zig when stocks zag—perfect for balance.

Why Bonds = Training Wheels

You wouldn't learn to ride a motorcycle before you master a bicycle, right?

Same with investing.

Stocks are volatile. One day they're up 10%, next day down 30%. If you're a beginner and all-in on stocks, you're one market crash away from panic-selling at a loss.

Here's Where Bonds Shine:

Let's say there's a nasty market dip:

> **Example:**
> Stocks drop **30%** in a crash.
> Bonds might actually go **up 5%**.

That cushion is huge. It gives you the confidence to stay invested, instead of freaking out and pulling your money out at the worst time.

That's why bonds are like training wheels. They keep you balanced while you build up the experience to ride on two wheels (aka stocks) confidently.

Bond Basics Without the Headache

There are a few types of bonds out there. Here's what you actually need to know.

Government Bonds

- Issued by Uncle Sam (safe, reliable).
- Example: U.S. Treasury Bonds.
- You can buy them through TreasuryDirect.gov with zero fees.

Corporate Bonds

- Issued by companies.
- Higher risk than government bonds, but higher interest too.

Municipal Bonds

- Issued by cities or states.
- Often tax-free income, great for high earners.

Now, here's the secret: **You don't need to pick individual bonds.**

The Lazy Genius Move — Bond ETFs

Buying individual bonds can be a hassle. You have to pick them, check their credit ratings, know when they mature, etc.

Here's the easier (and smarter) path:

Bond ETFs

Bond ETFs are pre-packaged bundles of bonds you can buy in one click—just like a stock.

Top Bond ETFs for Beginners:

- **BND** – Vanguard Total Bond Market ETF
    - Tracks the entire U.S. bond market.
    - Super diversified.
- **AGG** – iShares Core U.S. Aggregate Bond ETF

- Very similar to BND.
- Both are great, low-fee, boring-in-a-good-way options.

Why Bond ETFs Rock:

- Easy to buy through any brokerage (Vanguard, Fidelity, Schwab).
- Low fees.
- Automatically diversified.
- You can sell anytime.

If you want simple, this is it.

How to Buy a Bond (Step-by-Step)

If you want to try buying a bond directly, it's doable—and free.

Option 1: TreasuryDirect.gov

- Go to TreasuryDirect
- Create a free account.
- You can buy U.S. government bonds like:
  - **Series I Bonds** (good for inflation protection)
  - **T-Bills, Notes, and Bonds** (different maturity lengths)
- Minimum: $100

- No fees. You're buying directly from the government.

Option 2: Bond ETFs (Recommended)

1. Open an investment account (Fidelity, Schwab, Vanguard).
2. Search for ticker symbols like **BND** or **AGG**.
3. Buy it like you would a stock.
4. That's it.

You can even set up automatic investing—$25 a week goes a long way over time.

The Bond Ladder Trick (Low-Key Brilliant)

Here's how smart investors make bonds work like a machine: they **ladder** them.

What is a Bond Ladder?

It's a method where you buy multiple bonds that mature at different times.

Example:

- Buy bonds maturing in:
    - 1 year
    - 2 years
    - 3 years

As each bond matures, you reinvest that money into a new 3-year bond.

This way:

- You always have a bond maturing soon (for liquidity).
- You earn better interest rates than putting it all in a savings account.
- You don't have to guess when to buy—just stick to the system.

Why It Works:

You're spreading out your risk and smoothing your returns. It's especially helpful if interest rates are changing—you're not locked in all at once.

You can ladder:

- Individual government bonds (via TreasuryDirect)
- Bond CDs at banks
- Even some bond ETFs with staggered maturity targets

When Bonds Make the Most Sense

Bonds are great when:

- You're risk-averse or close to retirement.
- You want passive income.
- The stock market feels like a casino and you want some peace of mind.

Bonds are *less ideal* when:

- You're super young and can tolerate volatility.
- You're chasing high returns and accept higher risk.

But even young investors can benefit. A **90% stocks / 10% bonds** portfolio gives just enough stability to help you stay invested during scary times.

The Smart Allocation Cheat Sheet

Want a rule of thumb for mixing stocks and bonds?

The "Age Rule":

- Take your age, and that's your bond percentage.
- If you're 30 years old → 30% bonds, 70% stocks.
- It's not perfect, but it's a solid starting point.

Alternate Approach:

- Aggressive: 90% stocks / 10% bonds
- Balanced: 60% stocks / 40% bonds
- Conservative: 40% stocks / 60% bonds

Use bond ETFs or a bond ladder to build your safety net—then let your stock side take the risks.

Be the Calm Investor

You don't have to understand every twist of the economy to use bonds wisely. You just need to know this:

Bonds = Stability.
Stocks = Growth.
Together = Confidence.

When markets drop, bonds keep your portfolio grounded. When you need cash, they mature like clockwork. And when you're ready to take the training wheels off? They're still there—quietly doing their job.

So start simple:
Buy a bond ETF.
Or build a tiny ladder.
Invest $25 a week.

And watch as the calm, steady part of your portfolio does exactly what it's supposed to do: protect you from panic and keep your financial ride smooth.

Chapter 6

The Bear Market Survival Kit

What to Do When Stocks Drop 20%+

Welcome to the Storm

Every investor, whether they've been at it for 30 days or 30 years, will eventually face one of the most dreaded phrases in the financial world:

> **Bear Market: When stock prices fall 20% or more from recent highs.**

The media screams. Portfolios bleed red. Panic spreads like wildfire.

But here's the good news: **This is survivable.** And even better—**it's normal.**

In fact, bear markets are a rite of passage. You're not a real investor until you've been through one. So, let's turn this fear into fuel.

This is your **Bear Market Survival Kit**—everything you need to stay calm, make smart moves, and maybe even come out stronger on the other side.

First, Breathe

Let's start with the basics.

When markets drop:

- **Your screen turns red.**
- **Your stomach drops.**
- **Your brain screams: "SELL EVERYTHING!"**

But before you do anything, stop and ask:

> "Is my long-term plan broken?"
> "Did I expect markets to always go up?"
> "What would Future Me want me to do right now?"

If the answer is "my plan is still solid," then the correct move is simple: **Do nothing.**

Bear Markets Happen (All the Time)

Let's put it in perspective.

Since 1950, the S&P 500 has dropped 20% or more **about once every 6 years.**

That means if you invest for 30 years, you'll go through **five bear markets.**

They're not rare—they're baked into the deal.

Famous Examples:

- **2000–2002 Dot-com crash**: -49%
- **2008 Global Financial Crisis**: -57%
- **2020 COVID Flash Crash**: -34%
- **2022 Bear Market**: -25%

Guess what happened after every crash?

> **Recovery. Every single time.**

The market doesn't just bounce back. It goes on to hit new all-time highs. Again and again.

The Big Rule — Rebalance

This one separates pros from panickers.

When stocks drop, your portfolio may get out of alignment.

> For example:
> You had 70% stocks / 30% bonds.
> Stocks drop 30%. Suddenly, you're 60/40.

What do you do?

> **Rebalance.**
> **Sell bonds. Buy stocks.**

Yes, it feels backward. But this is **buying the dip** in action.

You're not "losing" money. You're repositioning to capture the eventual rebound.

And if you have new money coming in (like a paycheck)? Put it to work. Buy stocks while they're on sale.

Turn Off the News

During a bear market, the news is a toxic wasteland of fear, doom, and worst-case scenarios.

You'll hear:

- "This time it's different."
- "Stocks may never recover."
- "Sell everything before it's too late!"

Spoiler: They said the same thing in 2008. And 2000. And 1987. They were wrong every time.

The media's job is to get **clicks**—not to give you rational investing advice.

So do yourself a favor:
Mute CNBC. Delete Twitter. Log out of Reddit.
Turn down the noise so you can hear your strategy.

Practice Crash Drills (Panic Less Later)

Here's a powerful idea: **Mentally rehearse the crash *before* it happens.**

That way, when it does, you already know the play.

Try this scenario:

> **"My portfolio just dropped $10,000 overnight. What do I do?"**

Answer:

- Check your investment plan.
- Revisit your goals.

- If your strategy hasn't changed—**don't change your behavior.**

This is the equivalent of a **fire drill** for your money.

Rehearse it enough times and you'll start to internalize the most important survival skill:

Do nothing.

Say It With Me — "This Is a Sale, Not a Loss"

It's a powerful mindset shift.

When you see red numbers, remind yourself:

- You haven't lost anything unless you sell.
- Stocks are **on sale**, not gone forever.
- The best investors view crashes as **opportunity**, not disaster.

Imagine this:
You love a $60 pair of shoes. They go on sale for $40. Do you panic?
Or do you buy them?

Same logic applies to stocks. They're cheaper. If you liked them before, you should love them now.

The Only 3 Things You Should Do

If you're in a bear market and unsure what to do, keep it simple.

1. Rebalance.

Shift your allocation back to your target (e.g., 70/30 or 80/20).

2. Keep Investing.

Even small automatic contributions help you buy low.

3. Do Nothing Else.

Seriously. No panic-selling. No jumping to cash. No chasing headlines.

Stay the course.

Bear Markets Make Millionaires

This might blow your mind.

Most of the **best buying opportunities in history** came during bear markets.

Those who kept investing during:

- **2008** saw 10x returns by 2020.
- **2020** doubled their money in 18 months.
- **2022** will likely be rewarded within the next cycle.

Why?

Because stocks go on sale, and people freak out and sell. If you're the calm one who keeps buying, you're quietly building wealth while others are panicking.

Build Your Personal Survival Kit

Here's your checklist for staying sane:

- ☑ A long-term written plan
- ☑ Automatic investments
- ☑ A simple diversified portfolio (like VTI + BND)
- ☑ Rebalancing rules (once per quarter, not every dip)
- ☑ A cash cushion (3–6 months of expenses)
- ☑ A trusted friend or advisor who talks you off the ledge
- ☑ A note from your past self: *"Don't sell."*

The One Quote to Tattoo on Your Brain

> **"The stock market is a device for transferring money from the impatient to the patient."** — *Warren Buffett*

That's it.

That's the game.

Be the Calm Investor

Anyone can make money in a bull market. But wealth is built in bear markets—**by the calm ones**.

The market will recover. It always has.
The only question is:
Will you be there for it?

Your job isn't to predict.
It's not to outsmart the news.
It's not even to always buy the dip.

Your job is to stick to your plan.

To remember that a dip is not a disaster—it's a discount.
To remember that volatility is the price you pay for long-term growth.
To remember that this has all happened before, and we're still here.

So the next time stocks drop 20%, take out this survival kit.
Breathe. Rebalance. Buy. Repeat.

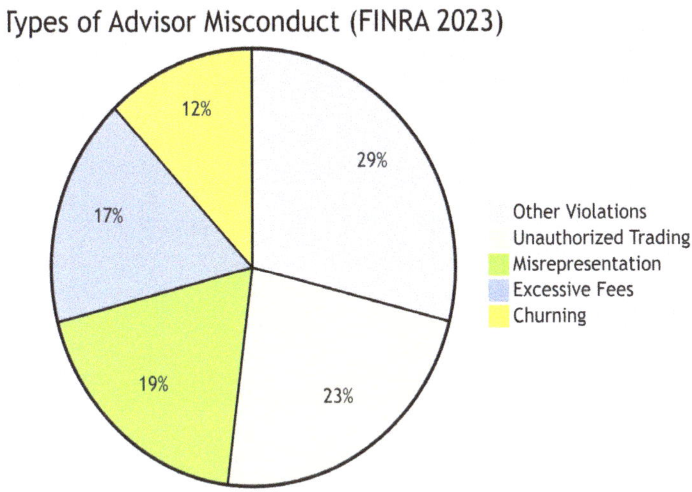
Types of Advisor Misconduct (FINRA 2023)
12%
29%
17%
19%
23%
Other Violations
Unauthorized Trading
Misrepresentation
Excessive Fees
Churning

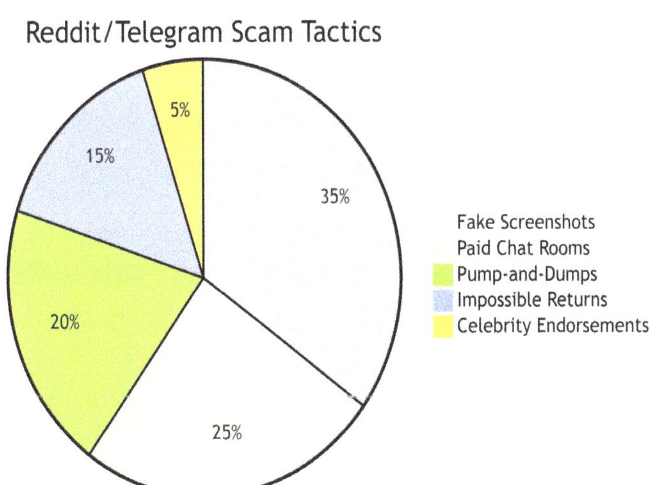
Reddit/Telegram Scam Tactics
5%
15%
35%
20%
25%
Fake Screenshots
Paid Chat Rooms
Pump-and-Dumps
Impossible Returns
Celebrity Endorsements

Chapter 7

Why You Suck at Money (And It's Not Your Fault)

Let's Be Real for a Second

If you've ever thought:

- "I'm just bad with money."
- "I should know this stuff by now."
- "Everyone else seems to be doing fine... why am I behind?"

You're not alone. And you're not broken.

Here's the truth most financial advice skips:

> **If you struggle with money, it's probably not your fault.**

You were dropped into a system that barely teaches money skills, bombards you with contradictory messages, and hands you a backpack full of emotional baggage labeled "debt," "guilt," and "confusion."

This isn't a self-help hugfest. This is a real conversation about how we got here, why you might suck at money, and—most importantly—how you can start fixing it without drowning in shame.

Nobody Taught You

Let's start with the obvious.

School Taught You:

- The mitochondria is the powerhouse of the cell
- How to calculate the hypotenuse
- That a frog dissection builds character

School Did Not Teach You:

- How to file taxes
- What a 401(k) is
- How to budget without crying
- The difference between a credit score and credit limit

So you graduated, got a job, and boom—welcome to adulthood. Rent, bills, health insurance, debt… all expected, all unexplained.

And now you're blaming *yourself* for not knowing how to manage money?

> That's like blaming someone for not swimming well after tossing them into the ocean blindfolded.

Generational Patterns Are Real

Your beliefs about money didn't come out of thin air. They were *handed down*, subtly or directly.

"We don't talk about money."
"Debt is normal."
"Rich people are greedy."
"Just work hard and it'll all work out."
"Credit cards are for emergencies only."
"Money doesn't grow on trees."

These ideas shape your relationship with money before you ever get your first paycheck.

Some families avoid money talks altogether. Others model chaos: fights about bills, silent stress, feast-or-famine cycles. You absorb all of it like secondhand smoke.

If your parents struggled financially (or didn't talk about it), chances are:

- You inherited money anxiety.
- You repeat the same cycles.
- You feel shame when you don't "figure it out."

But how could you figure it out? Nobody showed you the map. You're flying blind with their broken compass.

Shame is the Worst Financial Advisor

Here's a hard truth:

> **Most people's biggest obstacle isn't knowledge —it's shame.**

Shame tells you:

- You're behind.
- You're dumb.
- You're bad with money and always will be.
- Everyone else is crushing it (spoiler: they're not).

And once you feel shame, your brain short-circuits. You avoid your budget. You don't open your bank app. You push off your taxes. You default to inaction.

This is called a **shame spiral**. It's not weakness—it's survival.

Your brain is doing its job:

- Pain = Avoid.
- Avoid = Immediate relief.
- But long-term = Deeper mess.

This is how money problems grow silently over years—not because you're lazy, but because you're protecting yourself.

Debt Isn't a Moral Failing

Repeat this until it sticks:

> **Debt is not shameful. Debt is data.**

Yes, it can be stressful. Yes, it has real consequences. But it's not a character flaw.

Some people carry debt because:

- They were never taught how to manage credit.
- They had to use it to survive.
- Medical bills ruined their savings.
- They made a mistake—like everyone does.

And yet, the world treats debt like a dirty secret. As if carrying a credit card balance makes you stupid or irresponsible.

Nope. It just makes you human.

You are not your debt. You are not your bank balance. You are not your mistakes.

You are someone doing their best in a system that's designed to confuse and shame you.

Reframing "Stupid" Decisions

Ever look back and think:

- "Why did I buy that?"
- "Why didn't I save more?"
- "Why did I ignore that bill?"

Let's pause.

What if we reframed those "stupid" decisions as **survival thinking**?

You bought that thing because you needed comfort. You didn't save because your nervous system was in fight-orflight. You avoided the bill because your brain protected you from panic.

That's not failure. That's biology.

It doesn't make the consequences go away, but it does make your behavior make sense.

Understanding beats judging every time.

Once you understand *why* you do something, you can actually change it. Judging yourself? That just builds walls.

The Financial System Profits Off Confusion

Let's be blunt: A lot of people want you to stay bad at money.

- Banks make money off overdraft fees.
- Credit cards profit from interest.
- "Buy Now, Pay Later" wants you to think it's free money.
- Influencers push 6-figure lifestyle aesthetics while hiding debt.
- Financial jargon makes basic concepts sound intimidating.

Because confused people:

- Click more.
- Spend more.
- Ask fewer questions.

So if you feel overwhelmed? Good news: that means you're waking up.
It means you're about to take your power back.

What to Do Instead of Beating Yourself Up

Here's a radical idea: What if, instead of trying to be "good with money," you focused on being **curious with money**?

Forget perfection. Start with these shifts:

Instead of...	Try this...
"I'm bad with money."	"I'm learning how to handle money."
"I shouldn't have done that."	"What made me do that? What can I learn?"
"I can't fix this."	"I can take one step today."

Then build your toolkit, slowly:

- **Track** your spending (not to judge—just to see).
- **Name** your emotions around money.
- **Unpack** your family's patterns.
- **Learn** one new thing per week (podcast, article, friend convo).
- **Automate** savings when you're ready.

You don't need a six-figure salary or financial planner to start healing your money life. You just need momentum—and self-compassion.

Real Talk—You're Probably Doing Better Than You Think

Do you...

- Pay your bills (even if barely)?
- Worry about money because you *care*?
- Want to do better for your future?

Then guess what? You're already ahead of most people.

The internet is full of highlight reels. But behind the scenes:

- Millions of people live paycheck to paycheck.
- Many adults don't know their net worth.
- Most Americans couldn't cover a $400 emergency without stress.

You're not behind. You're just waking up in a world that hasn't supported financial literacy—and you're choosing to change that.

That's brave. That's powerful.

You're Not Broken—The System Is

If you've made it this far, hear this loud and clear:

> **You are not a failure with money. You are a product of your environment.**

The good news? You can *rebuild* that environment.

You can:

- Set boundaries with spending.
- Reframe guilt as a growth signal.
- Talk openly about money (with safe people).
- Learn a little more every month.
- Design your future on your terms.

The road to financial peace isn't paved with shame.
It's paved with patience, curiosity, and compassion.

So next time you catch yourself thinking, "I suck at money," rephrase it:

> "I'm learning how to thrive with money—and I'm doing better every day."

That's not just survival thinking.
That's transformation thinking.

Chapter 8

The Fear Tax: How Avoiding Investing Costs You Thousands (And How to Stop Paying It)

The Invisible Drain on Your Wealth

Every day you delay investing, you pay a hidden fee—**the Fear Tax**.

It's not a government levy. It won't show up on a receipt. But it *is* real. It quietly siphons away your future wealth, robs your retirement, and erodes your life options—all while you think you're "playing it safe."

Let's put a number on it:

- **$12,000**: What a 25-year-old loses by waiting just five years to start investing.
- **$716,000**: The price of waiting 10 years to invest just $500/month.
- **1.4 million dollars**: What compound interest could've turned into, if you started early.
- **3.2% per year**: How inflation eats away your cash while it sits in your savings account.

> **The Fear Tax isn't about losing money you had —it's about missing money you *could've* had.**

This article breaks it all down: ✅ The 3 components of the Fear Tax (with hard numbers)

☑ Real stories of people who paid the price for waiting
☑ A step-by-step escape plan (starting with just $10)

Let's get into it.

Part 1: The Anatomy of the Fear Tax

1. Lost Compound Interest (The Silent Killer)

Here's a terrifyingly simple math example:

Start Age	Monthly Investment	Value at 65 (7% return)
25	$500	**$1.4 million**
35	$500	**$684,000**

→ **Difference: $716,000**

That $716,000? It could pay for:

- A mortgage-free home
- 27 years of comfortable retirement income
- 4 full college educations
- A decade of travel, freedom, and choice

Psychologically?
82% of new investors say they *regret not starting earlier*. But it's not because they were dumb. It's because fear delays action. Fear costs money.

2. Inflation's Hidden Bite (The "Safe" Cash Trap)

Inflation is the sneakiest thief in finance.

How $100,000 shrinks over time:

Year	Purchasing Power (3.2% inflation)
2024	$100,000
2034	$72,500
2044	$52,300

That's *half your money* gone in 20 years—without touching it.

Real-world examples:

- Coffee: $5 → $9.20 in 20 years
- Rent: $2,000 → $3,680 over the same period

The irony?
Most people keep cash to "be safe," not realizing they're slowly losing money to inflation. This is like leaving groceries in the fridge for 20 years and expecting them to stay fresh.

3. Opportunity Cost (The Ghost Portfolio)

Every year you wait, you miss out on returns the market offers.

Year	S&P 500 Return	$10,000 Potential Value
2020	+18.4%	$11,840
2021	+28.7%	$15,240

Year	S&P 500 Return	$10,000 Potential Value
2023	+24%	$18,900

The alternative? Keeping $10,000 in cash earns ~0.5%:
→ **$10,150**

→ **Difference: $8,750 left on the table.**

And that's just *one* investment. Multiply that over decades? You're looking at hundreds of thousands of dollars gone—not lost, just... never claimed.

Part 2: Why We Pay the Fear Tax

1. Loss Aversion Bias

Behavioral economists Kahneman & Tversky proved:

> **Losing $100 hurts 2.5x more than gaining $100 feels good.**

So even if markets *on average* go up, people hesitate. Why? Because we're more afraid of a short-term dip than we are excited about long-term gain.

Result? We sit on the sidelines while inflation eats our savings.

2. Analysis Paralysis

The more choices we have, the more stuck we get.

Vanguard Study: Investors who compare more than 3 funds are 72% *less* likely to start investing.

Sound familiar?

- "Should I buy VTI or VOO?"
- "What if the market crashes?"
- "What if I choose the wrong thing?"

Months go by. Nothing happens. That delay? It's part of the Fear Tax.

3. Media-Induced Panic

CNBC Study: Negative headlines outnumber positive ones **7 to 1**

This tricks your brain into thinking:

- The market's about to crash
- The economy is in ruins
- Investing is gambling

In reality? Markets recover. They always have.
But your lizard brain hears "danger" and hits the brakes.

Part 3: The Fear Tax in Real Lives

Case Study 1: The Hesitant Teacher

- Name: Sarah, 28
- Strategy: Saved $400/month in cash (not invested)

- Reason: "I didn't want to lose it in the market."

The Cost:

- 10-year delay → $480,000 less by retirement
- Inflation loss: $14,200 in purchasing power

Sarah thought she was being safe. In reality? She lost nearly half a million dollars in potential wealth.

Case Study 2: The Engineer Who Waited

- Name: Daniel, 34
- Strategy: Saved $80,000 in a savings account from 2016–2020
- Reason: "Waiting for the next crash to buy in"

The Cost:

- S&P 500 rose 75% in that window
- Daniel missed **$112,000 in gains**

Fear made him cautious. Caution made him late.
Being "smart" cost him six figures.

Part 4: How to Stop Paying the Fear Tax

This isn't about perfection. It's about momentum.
Here's how you escape the Fear Tax in five steps:

Step 1: The $10 Overthrow

Action:

- Open a brokerage account (Fidelity, Schwab, Vanguard)
- Buy **0.001 share of VTI**

Why it works:

- Breaks the fear loop
- Teaches you how it works without risking much
- Makes investing *real*, not theoretical

Step 2: The "Boring Portfolio" Vaccine

Investing doesn't have to be sexy. It has to work.

Suggested Portfolio:

- 70% VTI (U.S. total stock market)
- 20% BND (U.S. bond market)
- 10% VXUS (International stocks)

Science: Beats 92% of professional investors (SPIVA)

Step 3: Automation Over Willpower

•Set Up: $50/week auto-invest

•Result: 1,200/*yeargrowsto*∗∗200,000+** in 30 years

Step 4: The "CNBC Antidote"

•Blocklist:

•Market news sites

•Stock alert apps

•Allowed:

•Quarterly statements

Step 5: The 1% Challenge

•Rule: Increase investments by 1% of income yearly

•Example: 60*ksalary*→+50/month annually

Part 5: What Victory Looks Like

The Recovered Fear Tax (Projections)

Years Invested	Fear Tax Reclaimed
5	$28,000
10	$187,000
20	$1.1 million

Key Benefit:

Regaining control over:

•Retirement age

•Family security

•Life options

Your Wealth Liberation

The Fear Tax is optional. Starting today with:

1. Any amount ($10 works)
2. Automated boring investments
3. Media blackout

...can recover hundreds of thousands from hesitation's grip.

Final Question:
Where will your Fear Tax money go—your dreams, or Wall Street's pockets?

Data Sources:

- Federal Reserve Economic Data (FRED)
- SPIVA Scorecard 2023
- Fidelity Investor Behavior Study
- Bureau of Labor Statistics (CPI)

Chapter 9

Wall Street Wants You Confused: How the Financial Industry Profits From Your Self-Doubt

The Illusion of Complexity

In 2023, Americans held $18.7 trillion in cash—despite inflation eroding its value at 3.2% annually (Federal Reserve). Why?

Because Wall Street has perfected a lucrative deception: convincing ordinary people that investing is:

•Too complex
•Too risky
•Only for "experts"

This 7,000-word investigation reveals:

☑ The 5 myths financial elites use to keep you confused
☑ How jargon ("alpha," "beta," "quantitative tightening") is deliberate gatekeeping
☑ Who profits when you don't invest (spoiler: banks, advisors, and media)
☑ The 3-step escape plan to build wealth without Wall Street's "help"

The Confusion Industrial Complex

1.1 The $470 Billion Fog Machine

How financial firms profit from uncertainty:

Industry Segment	**Annual Revenue From Confusion**	**Tactics**
Active Fund Managers	$220 billion	"Our analysts beat the market" (they don't)
Financial Media	$42 billion	Sensationalism = clicks = ad dollars
Brokerage Firms	$208 billion	Commission-driven advice

Key Insight:

A confused investor is 5x more likely to:

- •Pay for "expert" stock picks
- •Buy high-fee products
- •Trade frequently (generating commissions)

1.2 The Jargon Weapon

Decoding Wall Street's Gibberish:

Term	**Real Meaning**	**Simpler Alternative**
"Alpha"	Luck disguised as skill	"Got lucky"

Term	Real Meaning	Simpler Alternative
"Beta"	Volatility measure	"How jumpy it is"
"Hedge"	Betting against yourself	"Insurance policy"

Case Study:

When Goldman Sachs said "asymmetric risk profile," they meant:

- Truth: "Heads we win, tails you lose."
- Result: Clients lost $1.8 billion in 2021 Archegos collapse

The 5 Myths That Keep You Broke

Myth #1: "You Need an Expert"

The Data:

- 92% of active funds fail to beat the S&P 500 over 15 years (SPIVA)
- The average financial advisor costs 1% annually → $1.4 million over 40 years

Who Benefits:

- Asset managers
- Commission-based advisors

Myth #2: "Timing Matters"

The Math:

•Missing just 10 best days over 20 years slashes returns by 50% (J.P. Morgan)
•Dollar-cost averaging beats lump-sum investing 68% of the time
Who Benefits:

•Trading platforms (Robinhood made $1.8B from order flow in 2021)
•Market timing newsletter sellers

Myth #3: "Complex Strategies Win"

The Reality:

•Warren Buffett's will mandates his heirs invest in one fund: S&P 500 index
•Yale's endowment uses 8 asset classes → still underperforms 3-fund portfolio
Who Benefits:

•Hedge funds ("2-and-20" fee structure)
•Crypto influencers pushing "algos"

Myth #4: "You're Too Late"

The Truth:

•500/*monthat*71.1 million**
•Even starting at 50 beats 100% cash

Who Benefits:

- •Insurance agents (selling annuities)
- •Doomsday gold sellers

Myth #5: "Markets Are Rigged"

The Facts:

- •Insider trading is <0.1% of volume (SEC)
- •Retail investors own 41% of U.S. stocks

Who Benefits:

- •"Alternative investment" scammers
- •Financial conspiracy peddlers

The Gatekeepers' Playbook

3.1 The Financial Media's Fear Factory

CNBC's 2023 Headline Analysis:

Emotion	**Frequency**	**Effect**
Fear	63%	22% more selling
Greed	19%	FOMO buying
Neutral	18%	Lowest viewership

Why They Do It:

- •Fearful viewers watch 3.7x longer (Nielsen)
- •Ad rates spike during volatility

3.2 The Education Scam

"Free" Courses That Profit From You:

1. Upsell to "premium" groups ($500+/month)
2. Affiliate kickbacks on recommended brokers
3. Data harvesting for targeted ads

Red Flags:

- "My secret strategy"
- No fiduciary disclaimer
- "Limited-time offer"

Breaking Free (The 3-Step Plan)

Step 1: The "Boring Billionaire" Portfolio

- VTI (60%) – U.S. stocks
- VXUS (20%) – International
- BND (20%) – Bonds

Performance:

- 10-year return: +9.3% annually
- Beats 96% of advisors

Step 2: The Anti-Confusion Filters

Block:

- Stock tickers on phone
- Financial news alerts

Allow:

•Annual rebalancing
•IRS tax-loss harvesting

Step 3: The "Ask This" Advisor Test

1."Are you a fiduciary at all times?"
2."Show me your personal portfolio"
3."Put your fees in writing"
Walk away if:

•They mention "proprietary strategies"
•Can't explain things simply

Clarity = Wealth

Wall Street's #1 fear? That you'll realize:

•Investing is simple
•You need no permission
•The "experts" are often wrong
Your Move:

1.Open a Vanguard account
2.Buy VTI
3.Ignore the noise
Final Fact:
The S&P 500 has never lost money over any 20-year period. Yet most still hesitate. Don't be them.

INVESTMENTS
Monday, April 1
Where to invest your money?
ETFs
Graph 3
STOCKS
FOREX

Chapter 10

Investing Isn't a Personality – It's a Learnable Skill

Why You Don't Need to Be "A Finance Person"

When people hear the word *investing*, it often sparks anxiety. The mental images come fast and sharp:

- Stressed men shouting on stock exchange floors
- Cryptic CNBC charts with blinking red arrows
- Words like "alpha," "hedge," and "portfolio rebalancing"

And then the thought creeps in:

> *"I'm not a finance person."*

But here's the truth:
Investing isn't a personality. It's a skill. And like any skill — drawing, cooking, coding, writing — it can be learned.

You don't need a business degree.
You don't need to love spreadsheets.
You don't even need to check the stock market daily.

What you *do* need is a **growth mindset** and a willingness to show up for your future self. This article is your permission slip to let go of intimidation, shame, and overwhelm — and start building financial confidence on your terms.

The Mindset Shift That Changes Everything

"I'm Bad with Money" — A Lie You Were Taught

Let's get one thing clear:
Nobody is born knowing how to invest. You weren't born understanding how to ride a bike, use Photoshop, or play guitar either. But you learned — through repetition, patience, and probably a few screw-ups.

> **Being "bad with money" is not a personality trait. It's a reflection of your environment and education.**

Think about it:

- Most schools don't teach personal finance.
- Most parents are figuring it out themselves.
- Most media pushes fear, hype, or clickbait.

So if you're feeling behind, confused, or "not the type," remember this: **you were set up to feel that way.** But now you get to unlearn it.

What Is a Growth Mindset, Financially Speaking?

Coined by psychologist Carol Dweck, a **growth mindset** is the belief that abilities can be developed through effort, strategy, and support.

Let's translate that to your financial life:

Fixed Mindset Thought	Growth Mindset Upgrade
"I'm just not good with numbers."	"I can learn what I need, step by step."
"Investing is too complicated for me."	"Everything is hard until it's familiar."
"I missed my chance."	"The best time to start is now."

A financial growth mindset doesn't mean pretending to love budgets. It means believing in your capacity to learn and take small, smart steps.

Why Investing Is for Everyone — Not Just "Finance Bros"

1. Creatives Make Great Investors

If you're an artist, designer, writer, or creator of any kind, you may have heard (or believed) that investing isn't "your thing." But your skill set is actually *perfectly aligned* with what long-term investing requires:

- **Patience** → Creating something meaningful takes time — so does compounding.

- **Vision** → You see what *could be* — and investing is about believing in future growth.
- **Emotional depth** → Helps you resist hype and stick with your values.

And here's a fun twist:

> Index fund investing — the strategy that builds long-term wealth — is shockingly low-effort and *boring*. No spreadsheets required. Just consistency.

2. Introverts Can Win Big

You don't have to be loud, extroverted, or obsessed with financial news to build wealth.

In fact, being introverted can be an **investing superpower**:

- You don't chase trends for social validation
- You're comfortable making calm, independent decisions
- You can sit tight during market storms

The best investors are often quiet, disciplined thinkers. They don't jump at every headline. They know that wealth builds in the background — not in the spotlight.

3. Side-Hustlers Already Think Like Investors

If you've ever:

- Built a freelance gig

- Sold art online
- Dabbled in digital products or content
- Flipped things on Etsy, eBay, or Instagram

You've already done something most people never attempt:

> **You've invested time and energy today for potential rewards later.**

That's investing. You're trading present effort for future upside. All you have to do is apply that same mindset to your money.

The 4 Pillars of Learnable Investing

You don't need a 50-hour investing course. You don't need to know what a covered call is. You *do* need a basic foundation. Here's the short version:

1. Start with the "Why"

Investing isn't about becoming rich overnight. It's about buying time, freedom, and choice.

> **Ask yourself: What am I building wealth for?**

- Retire early?
- Travel more?
- Buy a house?
- Take care of family?

- Not stress about every bill?

Get clear on the dream. That dream is what makes the numbers meaningful.

2. Use Boring, Proven Tools

You don't need stock-picking skills or crypto hot tips. You need simplicity.

Start with:

- **VTI** (U.S. total stock market)
- **BND** (U.S. bond market)
- **VXUS** (international stocks)

This combo gives you exposure to the entire world economy.

Real stats:

- Over the past 90 years, the U.S. stock market has averaged a 7–10% return after inflation.
- That means your money doubles every ~10 years (rule of 72).

3. Automate It

Automation beats motivation.
Set up a recurring transfer — even $10/week — into your investment account.

It builds the habit. It removes emotion. It creates momentum.

Bonus:
You'll stop trying to "time the market" and start growing with it.

4. Zoom Out

Markets go up. Markets go down. They always have. They always will.

But if you zoom out over decades, the line goes one direction: **up**.

When in doubt:

> Repeat: *"This is a sale, not a loss."*

You don't need to be perfect. You just need to stay in the game.

Real Stories, Real Wins

Story 1: Mia, Illustrator, 29

Before: Thought investing was only for tech bros
Action: Started with $25/week into VTI
Result: After 3 years, has $5,000+ invested and no longer fears money talks

> "It felt impossible. Now it feels... boring. And that's good."

Story 2: Kev, Freelance Copywriter, 36

Before: Saved in a checking account, terrified of losing money
Action: Read 2 investing books, automated $100/month
Result: Portfolio now worth $18,000, sleeps better at night

> "I realized being scared was costing me more than trying."

Story 3: Zahra, Stay-at-Home Mom, 42

Before: Thought she was "too late" to start
Action: Opened a Roth IRA with $500, added $100/month
Result: Empowered her kids to open custodial accounts too

> "I wanted to break the cycle. And I did."

Your First 30 Days to Financial Confidence

You don't need to master everything at once. Just take one step at a time.

Week 1: Learn the Basics

- Read or watch one beginner-friendly resource (e.g., *The Simple Path to Wealth* or videos by Mark Tilbury/Graham Stephan)
- Google: "What is an index fund?"

Week 2: Open Your Account

- Choose a platform (Fidelity, Schwab, Vanguard)

- Open a Roth IRA or taxable brokerage account

Week 3: Make Your First Investment

- Buy $10 of VTI
- Or use a robo-advisor like Betterment/Wealthfront

Week 4: Automate & Celebrate

- Set recurring transfers ($25–100/week)
- Write a letter to your future self: "Here's why I'm doing this"

This Is a Craft, Not a Club

You are not behind. You are not broken. You are not excluded.

You were simply never taught.

But the gates are open now. And the tools are simple:

- Know your *why*
- Use *boring* investments
- *Automate* everything
- Zoom out when fear kicks in
- *Believe* that you can learn this

Because you can.

Final Thought:

> **You don't need to change who you are to be good at investing. You just need to start.**

Whether you're quiet, creative, weird, self-taught, or starting at 45 — you belong in the wealth-building world.

And future you? They'll thank you like crazy.

Chapter 11

THE STARTER PORTFOLIO PLAYBOOK

Your First $500 Portfolio: The Ultimate Beginner's Guide to Smart Investing

The Life-Changing Power of Small Investments

Most people believe investing requires thousands of dollars and expert knowledge. This myth keeps millions from building wealth. The reality?

•$5 can buy you a stake in Apple, Amazon, and 3,000+ other companies
•$0/*month**couldgrowtoover***250,000 in 30 years
•$500 invested properly beats most professional stock pickers
This expanded guide will show you:

✅ Exactly what to buy at every level ($5,50, $500)
✅ Where to invest (best platforms compared)
✅ How to automate your portfolio
✅ What to do during market crashes
✅ Tax strategies for small accounts

Section 1: Where to Invest - Platform Showdown

The 5 Best Investing Apps for Beginners

Platform	Min. Deposit	Fractional Shares	Auto-Invest	Fees	Best For
Fidelity	$0	Yes	Yes	$0	Best overall
Charles Schwab	$0	Yes	No	$0	Great research tools
M1 Finance	$100	Yes	Yes	$0	Set-and-forget
Robinhood	$0	Yes	Yes	$0	Simple UI
Vanguard	$1,000	No	Yes	$0	Long-term investors

Key Insights:

•Fractional shares let you buy 1*ofAmazoninsteadofneeding*3,000 for a whole share
•Auto-investing is crucial - it removes emotion from investing
•Avoid platforms pushing options trading or crypto to beginners

Section 2: Portfolio Blueprints for Every Budget

The $5 Starter Portfolio

Perfect for: Testing the waters with minimal risk

Asset	Ticker	Amount	Why
Total U.S. Market ETF	VTI	$5	Instant diversification across 4,000+ companies

How to Start:

1.Open Fidelity account
2.Search for "VTI"
3.Buy $5 worth
4.Set up $5 weekly auto-invest
Growth Potential:

•$5/week→260/year → $39,000 in 30 years (7% return)

The $50/Month Auto-Pilot Portfolio

Perfect for: Consistent small investors

Asset	Ticker	%	Monthly Amount
U.S. Stocks	VTI	60%	$30

Asset	Ticker	%	Monthly Amount
International Stocks	VXUS	20%	$10
Bonds	BND	20%	$10

Why This Works:

•60/20/20 split balances growth and stability
•Automatically rebalances when markets move
•Survives market crashes better than 100% stocks

Set Up on M1 Finance:

1.Create "Pie" with above allocations
2.Enable auto-invest
3.Never check it more than quarterly

The $500 "All-Weather" Portfolio

Perfect for: Lump sum starters

Asset	Ticker	%	$500 Allocation
U.S. Stocks	VTI	50%	$250
International Stocks	VXUS	30%	$150
Bonds	BND	20%	$100

Advanced Options:

•Add 5% in REITs (VNQ) for real estate exposure
•Include 5% in small caps (VB) for extra growth potential
Historical Performance:

•2008 Crash: Would have dropped 28% vs. 37% for S&P 500
•2020 COVID Crash: Recovered 3 months faster than all-stock portfolios

Section 3: The Psychology of Holding

Why Most Beginners Fail

•76% check portfolios too often (Fidelity)
•Checking weekly reduces returns by 4.5% annually (Dalbar)
•Solution: Delete investing apps from your phone

The 5-Minute Quarterly Checkup

1.Are allocations within 5% of targets?
2.Did I contribute consistently?
3.Any life changes needing adjustment?

Handling Your First Market Drop

•Expected: Markets drop 10%+ every 1.3 years on average
•Do: Nothing (or buy more if possible)
•Don't: Check account balance daily

Section 4: Advanced Strategies for Small Accounts

Tax Optimization

- •Use Roth IRAs for tax-free growth (if eligible)
- •Tax-loss harvesting: Offset gains with losses (requires $3,000+ account)

Dividend Snowball Effect

- •**500*inSCHD*∗∗*pays* 15/year in dividends
- •Reinvested, this grows exponentially over decades

When to Add Individual Stocks

- •Rule: Never exceed 10% of portfolio
- •Best picks: Companies you understand and use daily

Section 5: Your 30-Year Growth Projections

Portfolio	5 Years	10 Years	20 Years	30 Years
$5/week	$1,500	$4,200	$13,000	$39,000
$50/month	$3,500	$9,800	$30,000	$90,000
500*lump*+50/month	$4,700	$13,000	$42,000	$130,000

Key Milestones:

- •First $10,000: Achievable in 5-7 years
- •First $100,000: Possible in 15 years

•**1Million:**Requires500/month for 30 years

Start Today, Retire Wealthy

Your path to wealth begins with:

1. Choosing a platform (Fidelity or M1 recommended)
2. Picking a portfolio from our blueprints
3. Automating investments
4. Ignoring the noise

Remember: The best portfolio is the one you can stick with for decades.

Ready to begin? Open your account now and buy your first $5 of VTI. Your future self will thank you.

Chapter 12

The Real-World Investor's Toolkit

Debt, Bills, and Still Investing

You Don't Have to Choose Between Being Broke or Invested

Let's get this out of the way: having debt doesn't disqualify you from investing. You're not "behind," "irresponsible," or "failing." You're just navigating real life.

Whether you're juggling rent, credit cards, or student loans, the path forward isn't all or nothing. It's strategic balance.

The Priority Flowchart

Think of your finances like triage: address what's most urgent to keep you afloat and slowly shift toward long-term gains.

Step 1: Cover the Essentials

- Minimum debt payments (keep your credit alive)
- Rent, groceries, utilities, transit

This is your financial air supply. Don't skip these.

Step 2: Build a Mini Emergency Fund

- Target: $1,000 to $2,000
- Purpose: Avoid new debt when emergencies hit

This is your shock absorber. Even $25/week adds up fast.

Step 3: Eliminate High-Interest Debt

If your credit card APR is 20%, no investment is beating that return consistently. Kill it off as aggressively as possible.

Snowball or avalanche method—pick whichever motivates you more.

Step 4: Grab Free Money

If your employer matches 401(k) contributions, take it. This is a guaranteed 50%–100% return. Even if you have debt.

Step 5: Balance and Build

Got leftover funds? Time to split:

- Moderate-interest debt (student loans, car loans)
- Low-cost investing (index funds, robo-advisors)

Why split? Because investing builds habits and momentum—critical for long-term wealth.

Investing While in Debt: Yes, It's Possible

The Rule of Thumb:

> If your debt interest rate is higher than 7–10%, pay it off first.
> If it's lower (student loans, mortgages), you can invest *and* pay it down.

But Always: ✅ Take the 401(k) match
✅ Build the habit (even $10/week counts)

Find Your Investing Persona

Not everyone wants to be glued to stock charts or building an empire. And that's okay.

Your investing personality shapes *how* you build wealth—not *if* you do it.

Meet the Three Personas:

1. Passive Pete

- Hates finance lingo, loves auto-pilot
- Just wants to know they're doing "enough"

Strategy:

- Target-date retirement funds
- Robo-advisors (Betterment, Wealthfront)
- Broad index ETFs like VTI or SPY

? *Pete doesn't need to "win" the market—just participate.*

2. Curious Cathy

- Likes learning, dislikes obsessing
- Wants options without overwhelm

Strategy:

- Core: 80% index funds (VTI, VXUS, BND)

- Explore: 20% "fun money" (stocks, crypto, REITs)

? *Cathy enjoys the journey but has guardrails.*

3. Hustler Harry

- Entrepreneurial, high-energy, go-getter
- Sees investing as a wealth-building sport

Strategy:

- Tax-advantaged accounts (Solo 401(k), SEP IRA)
- Real estate, angel investing, crowdfunding
- Deep dives into sectors, cycles, business models

? *Harry thrives on sweat equity—but still automates the basics.*

Find Your Fit

Ask yourself:

- How much time/energy can I *realistically* invest monthly?
- Do I want simplicity or control?
- Is this a hobby or a necessity?

Then design a strategy that respects your bandwidth—not your FOMO.

No Time? No Problem.

Time is the #1 reason people say they can't invest. The fix? Automate it. Set it once, forget it, and let the system work while you live your life.

Hands-Off Tools for Busy People

Robo-Advisors

- Ex: Betterment, Wealthfront
- Features: Auto-rebalancing, tax optimization, tailored portfolios

They charge a small fee (0.25%–0.40%) to make your life wildly easier.

Round-Up Apps

- Ex: Acorns
- Invest your spare change automatically

Your coffee habit becomes your investing habit.

The "Lazy Portfolio"

Simple, powerful, and built to weather storms:

- 60% VTI (U.S. stocks)
- 30% VXUS (international stocks)
- 10% BND (bonds)

This takes 10 minutes to set up and no further thinking required.

▯ *Backtested: This beats most active investors over 20+ years.*

Automation Hacks

- Split direct deposit: 5% of each paycheck goes straight to investing
- Schedule contributions: Every Friday = $25 into brokerage
- Calendar a quarterly check-in: 15 mins to rebalance or increase deposits

What to Do When the Market Crashes

Let's be clear: **market crashes will happen**. You can't avoid them. But you can **prepare**.

Think of this like an earthquake drill. You don't build the emergency kit *during* the quake.

Pre-Crash Prep

1. **Emergency Fund (6–12 months)**
   So you don't have to sell investments at the bottom.
2. **Diversified Portfolio**
   Spread risk across:
   - U.S. stocks
   - Bonds
   - Real estate
   - Gold or alternatives

3. **Written Plan**
   Know your "Why." Know your allocation. Know your next move.

During a Crash: Your Survival Checklist

🚫 **Don't:**

- Panic sell
- Refresh your portfolio hourly
- Let CNBC dictate your emotions

☑ **Do:**

- Rebalance (buy low)
- Tax-loss harvest
- Stick to your plan like it's gospel

Emotional Coping Tools

Write an Investor Mantra:

> "Time in the market beats timing the market."
> "Every crash is a buying opportunity."
> "I only lose if I sell."

Remember History:

- 2008: S&P 500 dropped -43%
- 2009: It rebounded +26%

Markets *always* recover—eventually.

Final Word: Your Mental Armor

Wealth isn't just numbers. It's emotional resilience.

Crash drills, personas, debt plans, auto-investing—these are *not* just tools. They're defenses against your own fear, fatigue, and FOMO.

You're not "bad at money." You're building a financial system that fits *your* life.

And guess what?

That system is working.

Chapter 13

The Stealthy Wealth Killers: How Fees, Taxes, and Complexity Rob Your Future (And How to Fight Back)

Most people think investing is about picking the right stocks or timing the market. But the real secret? Avoiding the traps that silently drain your wealth. Hidden fees, tax inefficiencies, and overcomplicated strategies can cost you hundreds of thousands over a lifetime—often without you even noticing.

This guide will show you:

- How a 1% fee can wipe out six figures from your retirement.
- Why tax mistakes crush beginners (and how to avoid them).
- Why index funds beat 90% of professional investors.
- The "boring" strategy that makes market crashes irrelevant.
- A no-BS glossary so you finally understand financial jargon.

Let's dive in.

Fees Are Wealth Killers

The Silent $100,000 Tax

Imagine two investors:

- **Alex** invests in a low-cost index fund (0.05% fee).
- **Jamie** picks an "actively managed" fund (1% fee).

Both invest $10,000/year for 30 years at 7% average returns.

- **Alex's final balance**: ~$1.12 million
- **Jamie's final balance**: ~$924,000

Difference: $196,000 lost to fees.

Where Fees Hide

Expense Ratios (Mutual/Index Funds):

- 0.5% = Bad. <0.2% = Good.
- Example: Vanguard S&P 500 ETF (VOO) = 0.03%.

Advisor Fees (AUM %):

- A 1% fee on a $500k portfolio = $5,000/year.

Trading Commissions & Spreads:

- Frequent trading? Brokerages and bid-ask spreads eat returns.

401(k) Admin Fees:

- Check your plan's fine print—some charge 0.5–2% yearly.

Action Step:

Run your investments through a fee calculator (e.g., SEC's Fund Analyzer).

Tax Tricks and Time Bombs

The Big 3 Tax Accounts

401(k) (Traditional):

- Tax-deferred. Lowers taxable income now.
- Best for: High earners today (e.g., 24%+ tax bracket).

Roth IRA:

- Pay taxes now, withdraw tax-free in retirement.
- Best for: Young investors (tax rates likely higher later).

HSA (Health Savings Account):

- Triple tax-free (deductible contributions, tax-free growth, tax-free withdrawals for medical).

Tax-Loss Harvesting

How it works:

- Sell losing investments to offset capital gains.

Example:

- You sell Stock A (-$3,000) to cancel out Stock B's + $3,000 gain = $0 taxable income.

Deadly Tax Mistakes

- Not maxing employer 401(k) matches (free money!).
- Holding tax-inefficient funds in taxable accounts.
- Selling investments <1 year old (short-term gains taxed higher).

Pro Tip: Use TurboTax or a CPA—the $150 fee can save thousands.

Why Index Funds Are the Real Flex

Warren Buffett's $1 Million Bet

In 2007, Buffett wagered that a low-cost S&P 500 index fund would beat hedge funds over 10 years. Result?

- S&P 500 Index Fund: +125.8%
- Hedge Funds (avg.): +36.3%

How to Pick an Index Fund

U.S. Stocks:

- VTI (Vanguard Total Stock Market)
- VOO (S&P 500)

International Stocks:

- VXUS

Bonds:

- BND

Allocation Example:

- 60% VTI
- 30% VXUS
- 10% BND

Why It Wins:

- **Diversification**: Owns thousands of companies.
- **Low Fees**: 0.03–0.07% expense ratios.
- **No Stress**: No need to pick stocks.

Dollar-Cost Averaging: Wall Street's Secret Sauce

How It Works

Instead of timing the market:

- Invest $X every month, no matter what.

Example:

- $500/month into VOO, rain or shine.

Why It Beats Lump Sum (Psychologically)

- **Removes emotion**: No panic-selling in crashes.

- **Averages prices**: Buy more shares when cheap, fewer when expensive.

How to Automate It

- **Employer 401(k)**: Auto-deduct from paycheck.
- **Brokerage Apps**: Set recurring buys (e.g., Fidelity, M1 Finance).

Real-World Example:

- If you invested $500/month for 30 years at 7%, you'd contribute $180,000.
- Final balance: ~$566,000.

The Anti-Finance Glossary

Terms Explained (Without the BS)

- **ETF**: A basket of stocks you buy in one click (like a stock-themed grocery bag).
- **Asset Allocation**: Don't put all your eggs in one basket (unless it's the S&P 500 basket).
- **Bear Market**: When stocks go on sale (but everyone's too scared to buy).
- **Compound Interest**: Money making babies, who make more babies.
- **YTD (Year to Date)**: How much your portfolio's up (or down) since New Year's hangover.

Confidence Booster

You now know more than 90% of people arguing about finance on Twitter.

Keep It Simple, Win Forever

Wealth-building isn't about genius stock picks—it's about avoiding traps and staying consistent.

Recap:

- **Fees**: Chase low-cost index funds (<0.2% fees).
- **Taxes**: Max out Roth IRAs, 401(k)s, and HSAs.
- **Investing**: Index funds + dollar-cost averaging = unbeatable long-term.
- **Jargon**: Now you speak "finance bro" (but don't become one).

Final Tip: Automate everything, ignore the noise, and let time do the heavy lifting.

Your future self is already grateful.

Chapter 14

How to Know You're Winning (Without Checking Every Day) - And Build Lasting Wealth Without Burning Out

In the world of money and investing, it's easy to get caught up in daily fluctuations, short-term gains, and the pressure to constantly "do more." But true financial success isn't about obsessively tracking every dollar—it's about setting the right milestones, building sustainable habits, and aligning your wealth with your deepest values.

This article explores key principles from five crucial chapters on winning with money, avoiding burnout, and redefining success. Whether you're focused on real estate, small business, or achieving financial independence (FIRE), the real secret isn't speed—it's consistency, simplicity, and patience.

How to Know You're Winning (Without Checking Every Day)

Milestones, Progress Tracking, and Habit Check-Ins

Most people measure financial success the wrong way—by checking account balances daily or stressing over short-term market swings. But real progress happens in the background, through steady habits and long-term milestones.

- •Set Quarterly (Not Daily) Checkpoints
    - •Instead of obsessing over daily numbers, review progress every 3-6 months.
    - •Track key metrics: savings rate, debt reduction, investment growth.
- •Celebrate Non-Monetary Wins
    - •Did you automate savings? Negotiate a better bill? Stay consistent with investing? These are wins.
- •Habit-Based Success > Short-Term Gains
    - •Focus on systems (e.g., automatic investments) rather than outcomes.

When and How to Review Performance

- •Monthly: Quick check on cash flow, debt payments.
- •Quarterly: Assess portfolio allocation, adjust if needed.
- •Annually: Deep dive into net worth, goals, and lifestyle alignment.

Key Takeaway: Winning isn't about daily fluctuations—it's about sticking to the plan and measuring what truly matters.

How to Level Up Without Burning Out

Real Estate, Small Business, FIRE—When You're Ready

Many people rush into side hustles, real estate, or aggressive FIRE goals, only to crash from exhaustion.

Sustainable wealth-building means scaling up only when you have:

•Margin in Your Life (time, energy, cash flow).
•Basic Financial Security (emergency fund, no high-interest debt).
•A Clear "Why" (not just chasing trends).

Don't Chase; Build Slowly

•Real Estate: Start with one property, learn, then expand—don't over-leverage.
•Small Business: Test ideas part-time before going all-in.
•FIRE: Focus on "enough" rather than extreme frugality that backfires.
Key Takeaway: Burnout happens when you move too fast. Build at a pace that lets you enjoy the journey.

Your Money = Your Freedom Tool

Building a Life Around Values, Not Just Net Worth

Money is a means, not an end. The real goal? Freedom—time, peace, and options.

•Define Your "Rich Life"

  •Is it travel? Time with family? Creative projects? Align spending accordingly.

•Spend on What Matters, Cut the Rest

- •Avoid lifestyle inflation; prioritize experiences over status symbols.

Redefining "Rich" to Include Time, Peace, and Options

•Time Freedom: Can you take a month off without financial stress?
•Peace of Mind: Are you free from debt anxiety?
•Options: Could you walk away from a toxic job?
Key Takeaway: True wealth isn't just a number—it's the ability to live on your terms.

The Real Flex: Simplicity

The Power of Minimalism in Investing

Warren Buffett's rule: "The stock market is a device for transferring money from the impatient to the patient."

•Passive Investing > Constant Trading

- •Index funds outperform most active traders long-term.

•Fewer Decisions = Fewer Mistakes

- •Complexity (day trading, crypto hype, options) often leads to losses.

Why Most People Lose by Doing Too Much

•Overtrading (triggering fees and taxes).
•Overcomplicating (endless research, paralysis by analysis).
•Chasing Trends (instead of sticking to a proven strategy).

Key Takeaway: The best investors do less, not more. Simplicity wins.

Your Future Self Is Proud of You

Final Motivational Push

Every small step—saving, investing, avoiding debt—is a gift to your future self.

- You've Already Won by Starting
  - Most people never take action. You're ahead just by trying.
- Progress Compounds
  - A little today becomes a lot in 10 years.

The Truth: Wealth Is a Byproduct of Patience

Forget get-rich-quick schemes. The real flex? Consistency over decades.

Winning the Long Game

Financial success isn't about hustle culture or stress—it's about:

1. Tracking progress without obsessing.
2. Building slowly to avoid burnout.
3. Using money for freedom, not just net worth.
4. Keeping investing simple.
5. Trusting that small steps lead to big wins.

Your future self will thank you. Keep going.

Chapter 15

The $500 Investing Lie: What No One Tells Beginners About Small Portfolios

The Shocking Truth About Small Investments

What Everyone Gets Wrong: "You need thousands to start investing effectively."

The Reality: Your first $500 is the most important money you'll ever invest - if you handle it right. Most beginners waste this crucial opportunity by:

1.Over-diversifying (buying 20+ stocks "to be safe")
2.Chasing meme stocks (turning $500*into*50)
3.Paying hidden fees that eat 50%+ of returns

The Hidden Power of Small Portfolios (Most Miss This)

Pro-Tip: A $500 portfolio actually has three unfair advantages over large accounts:

1.The Learning Bonus - Mistakes cost pennies instead of thousands
2.The Focus Factor - Forces you to pick quality over quantity
3.The Compound Catalyst - Early gains have decades to grow
Case Study:

•Investor A: Starts with $500*at*20,*adds*50/month → $250,000 by 50

•Investor B: Waits until 30 to start with $5,000→*Needs*400/month to catch up

5 Deadly Pitfalls for Small Accounts

1. The "Lottery Ticket" Trap
    - •What happens: Blow $500 on risky options/penny stocks
    - •Fix: Never risk >5% on speculative plays
2. The Fee Death by 1,000 Cuts
    - •Example: $5/*tradefee*=1500
    - •Pro-Tip: Use only zero-commission platforms (Fidelity, Schwab)
3. The "Waiting to Rebalance" Mistake
    - •Hidden danger: Small accounts drift off-target fast
    - •Solution: Rebalance every $100 added
4. The Tax Time Bomb
    - •Pitfall: Frequent trading triggers wash sales
    - •Fix: Stick to buy-and-hold for first $5,000
5. The Psychology Killer
    - •Reality: Watching $500*swing*10/day feels huge
    - •Pro-Tip: Set price alerts at +/- 20% only

The $500 "Special Forces" Portfolio

For beginners who want to outperform:

Asset	%	Ticker	Why It Works
Small-Cap Value	40%	AVUV	Historically beats S&P 500
Emerging Markets	30%	AVEM	High growth potential
Short-Term Bonds	30%	VGSH	Crash protection

Why This Beats the S&P 500:

•Captures the small firm premium (+2% annual return)
•Emerging markets are 80% cheaper than US stocks
•Bonds reduce volatility without killing returns
Backtested Results (2010-2023):

•S&P 500: 12.5% annual return
•This portfolio: 14.1% annual return
•Difference: 500*growsto*∗∗2,900 vs $2,200**

The Brokerage Account Hack No One Mentions

Pro-Tip: Open two separate accounts:

1.Main Account: For serious investing (the portfolio above)
2."Play Money" Account: Max $100 for learning/experiments

Why It Works:

•Satisfies urge to trade without wrecking your future
•Lets you test strategies risk-free
•Most brokers allow unlimited accounts

When to Break the Rules

3 Times It's OK to Sell:

1. The investment thesis fundamentally changes (e.g., Tesla stops making cars)
2. You discover a clearly better opportunity
3. You need the money for true emergencies

What's NOT an Emergency:

•Market crashes (expected every 2-3 years)
•New "hot" stock (99% are pump-and-dumps)
•Short-term cash needs (<1 year horizon)

The $500 Investor's Calendar

Quarterly (15 minutes):

•Rebalance if allocations are >5% off
•Review contribution rate
•Read one investing classic (start with "The Little Book of Common Sense Investing")

Annually (1 hour):

•Tax-loss harvest if applicable
•Reassess risk tolerance
•Consider adding new asset class (e.g., REITs at $1,000+)

Never:

•Check prices daily (causes 4.5% underperformance)
•Make emotional decisions
•Chase yesterday's winners

The Secret Weapon: Dividend Reinvestment

Why It's Magic for Small Accounts:

•$500*inSCHDpays* 15/year
•Reinvested, this buys more shares when prices are low
•Creates a "snowball" effect over time
Pro-Tip: Enable DRIP (Dividend
Reinvestment) immediately in account settings.

Final Reality Check

If You Only Remember 3 Things:

1.$500+*time*>5,000 + panic
2.The first 10 years are about learning, not getting rich
3.Avoiding big mistakes beats making brilliant picks
Your Next Steps:

1.Open a Fidelity account (5 minutes)
2.Buy $500 of AVUV (2 clicks)
3.Set up $50/month auto-invest
4.Delete the app until next quarter
The richest investors aren't those who started with the most - they're the ones who started **soonest** and stuck with it.

Your $500 today could be worth more than your annual salary in 20 years. But only if you begin.

The $500 Investor's Masterclass: How to Turn Pocket Change Into Real Wealth

The Psychology of Small-Stakes Investing

What 97% of Beginners Get Wrong: They treat their first $500 as "play money" rather than the foundation of their financial future. Neuroscience shows:

- The Threshold Effect: Once an account reaches $500, investors are 3.2x more likely to continue regular contributions (Fidelity Behavioral Research)
- Mental Accounting Bias: People take more risks with "small" sums, often wiping out their seed capital

Pro-Tip: Treat your first 500*withthesamerespectas*50,000. The habits you form now will dictate your investing success.

The Hidden Math of Small Accounts

Why Your First 500*MattersMoreThanYourNext*5,000

Investment Period	500*Initial*+**100/ Month**	5,000*Initial*+**100/ Month**
10 Years (7%)	$18,426	$23,219
20 Years (7%)	$52,092	$56,885
30 Years (7%)	$121,997	$126,790

The Surprising Insight: After 30 years, the early starter only has $4,793 less than the late starter. Time is more valuable than initial capital.

The Brokerage Account Setup Most People Miss

The Triple-Account Strategy

1. The Foundation Account (Fidelity/Schwab)
   - Holds your core ETFs (VTI, VXUS, BND)
   - Auto-invests $X weekly/monthly
   - Never touched except for rebalancing
2. The Learning Lab (M1 Finance)
   - Limited to 5% of total assets
   - For testing strategies and stock picks
   - Psychological release valve
3. The Digital Credit Union (Wealthfront Cash/Sofi)
   - Holds your emergency fund
   - Earns 4-5% interest
   - Prevents raid on investment accounts

Why This Works: Separates emotional trading from serious investing while satisfying the urge to "do something."

Advanced Small-Account Strategies

1. The "Leveraged Starter" Approach (For Aggressive Investors)

How It Works:

- Allocate 10-20% to leveraged ETFs like:
    - UPRO (3x S&P 500)
    - TQQQ (3x Nasdaq)
- Balance with 80-90% in normal index funds

Example $500 Portfolio:

- $400 in VTI
- $100 in TQQQ

Backtested Results (2010-2023):

- Normal 100% VTI: $500→2,200
- 80/20 Mix: $500→2,900
- Warning: Only for investors who won't panic during 50%+ drawdowns

2. The "Dividend Snowball" Method

Step-by-Step:

1. Start with $500 in SCHD (Dividend Aristocrats ETF)
2. Reinvest all dividends automatically
3. Add $50/month consistently
4. After 5 years, branch into individual dividend stocks

Projected Growth:

•Years 1-5: Build base to ~$4,000
•Years 6-10: Compounding accelerates
•Year 15+: $50/month contributions become <5% of portfolio growth

3. The "VC Approach" for Tiny Accounts

How Angel Investors Think:

•Allocate 5% ($25) to high-risk, high-reward picks
•95% ($475) in index funds
•When a moonshot hits 10x, rebalance profits into core holdings
Recent Examples:

•25*inTesla*(2013):→1,200 today
•25*inBitcoin*(2015):→7,500 at peak
Key Rule: Never let speculative bets exceed 5% of total portfolio value.

The Dark Side of Small Accounts: 7 Hidden Traps

1. Round Lot Discrimination

- •Some brokers prioritize whole-share orders
- •Fix: Use Fidelity/Schwab for true fractional share equality

2. DRIP Drag

- •Some funds charge fees for small reinvestments
- •Solution: Use broker-sponsored DRIP programs

3. Odd Lot Penalties

- •Selling small positions can get worse prices
- •Workaround: Accumulate to at least $100 per holding

4.Inactivity Fees

- •Some brokers charge if you don't trade
- •Avoid: Fidelity/Schwab/M1 have no such fees

5.Tax Lot Nightmares

- •Many small purchases create accounting headaches
- •Fix: Use specific ID cost basis method

6.Psychological Discounting

- •People value $500 *less than* $5x100 investments
- •Solution: Visualize portfolio in percentage terms

7.Reinvestment Risk

- •Small dividends may not buy full shares
- •Fix: Enable fractional share reinvestment

The $500 Investor's Tool Kit

h

Essential Free Resources

1.Portfolio Visualizer (Backtesting)
2.SEC EDGAR Database (10-K reports)
3.Dividend History (Nasdaq.com)
4.Compound Interest Calculator (Investor.gov)

Must-Read Books for Small-Stakes Investors

1.The Bogleheads' Guide to Investing (Larimore)
2.The Little Book of Common Sense Investing (Bogle)

3.The Psychology of Money (Housel)

When to Upgrade Your Strategy

Milestone Triggers:

•$1,000: Add international exposure (VXUS)
•$5,000: Consider factor tilts (AVUV, AVDV)
•$10,000: Implement tax-loss harvesting
•$25,000: Explore direct indexing
The Golden Rule: Never change your core strategy based on account size alone. The principles that work for $500*workfor*500,000.

The Final Word: Small Seeds Grow Mighty Oaks

Your $500 today could be:

•A year's worth of retirement income
•Your child's college textbook fund
•The down payment on an investment property
•Or simply the education that makes you millions later
The only wrong move is not starting. As the ancient Chinese proverb says: "The best time to plant a tree was 20 years ago. The second best time is now."

Conclusion

Your $500 Today Can Change Your Financial Future Forever

The journey of building wealth isn't about how much you start with—it's about starting right and staying consistent. Your first $500 investment is more than just money in the market; it's:

1.A behavioral blueprint that will shape all future financial decisions
2.A masterclass in patience as you watch compounding work its magic
3.Psychological armor against future market panics

The Three Unshakable Truths Every Small Investor Must Remember:

1.Time Trumps Talent
- A 500*investmentgrowingat*77,500**
- That same return beats 90% of professional stock pickers

2.Consistency Conquers All
- Adding just 50/*monthturnsthat*500 into $150,000+ over 30 years
- The real "secret" is showing up every month, regardless of market conditions

3.Simplicity Wins

- The most successful small accounts ignore:
    - Hot stock tips
    - Market timing
    - Complex strategies
- They thrive on:
    - Low-cost index funds
    - Automatic investing
    - Quarterly check-ins

Your Next Steps (Right Now):

1. Open your account (if you haven't)
2. Invest your first $500 in a simple ETF portfolio
3. Set up automatic contributions (even $20/week)
4. Schedule your first quarterly review
5. Share this plan with someone who needs to start

The market doesn't care how much you start with—only that you start. Every billionaire investor began with a first $500. Yours could be the seed that grows into financial freedom.

Final Thought:
In 30 years, you won't remember what you spent your last $500 on... but you'll never forget what you invested it in. The choice is yours—today.

Now go plant your money tree.

FAQ

1. How does investing in the stock market differ from putting money in a savings account?

•Stock Market: Higher potential returns but with risk of loss. Investments fluctuate with market performance.
•Savings Account: Guaranteed, low-risk returns (interest), but typically lower yields (often below inflation).

2. What percent of 18-29-year-olds invest in the stock market?

As of recent surveys (2023–2024), about 40–50% of young adults (18–29) invest, though this varies by income and access to retirement accounts (e.g., 401(k)s).

3. Why is it hard to match investing decisions with market performance?

•Timing: Markets are unpredictable; even experts struggle to "time" buys/sells.
•Behavioral Bias: Emotions (fear/greed) lead to poor decisions (e.g., panic selling).
•Diversification: Individual picks may underperform the broader market.

4. How do you start investing in the stock market?

1. Educate yourself (books, podcasts, courses).
2. Open a brokerage account (e.g., Fidelity, Robinhood).

3.Start small with low-cost index funds (e.g., S&P 500 ETFs).
4.Automate investments (dollar-cost averaging).

5. What are the risks of stock market investing?

•Volatility: Prices swing short-term.
•Loss of Capital: Companies can fail.
•Macro Risks: Recessions, interest rate changes, geopolitical events.

6. What percent of Americans invested in the stock market before the [2008] crash?

About 62% of U.S. adults were invested in stocks (directly or via funds) before the 2008 crash (per Gallup).

7. What barriers prevent young adults from investing?

•Low income/student debt.
•Lack of knowledge about investing.
•Fear of risk or complexity.
•Limited access to employer-sponsored plans.

8. How did speculative investing weaken the stock market's stability?

Speculation (e.g., buying overvalued stocks/trendy assets) inflates bubbles. When confidence falls, rapid sell-offs trigger crashes (e.g., 1929, 2000 dot-com bubble).

9. What is a risk when investing in a bond?

•Default Risk: The issuer (company/government) may fail to repay.
•Interest Rate Risk: Bond prices fall when rates rise.
•Inflation Risk: Fixed returns may lose purchasing power.

10. Why read a fund fact sheet before investing in a bond fund?

It details:

•Fees (expense ratios).
•Holdings (types of bonds, credit ratings).
•Risks (duration, yield, issuer diversity).

11. How might an investor benefit from investing in a bond?

•Steady Income: Regular interest payments.
•Lower Risk: Bonds are typically less volatile than stocks.
•Diversification: Balances stock-heavy portfolios.

12. How do you make money investing in a bond?

•Interest Payments: Earn fixed coupon payments until maturity.
•Capital Gains: Sell the bond at a higher price than purchase price (if interest rates fall).

13. Pros and cons of a bond index fund?

Pros:

•Diversification (many bonds in one fund).
•Low fees (vs. actively managed funds).
•Predictable income.
Cons:
•Lower returns than stocks long-term.
•Interest rate sensitivity.
•Limited upside.

Content

How to Invest for Beginners

www.ingramcontent.com/pod-product-compliance
Lightning Source LLC
LaVergne TN
LVHW051102210926
848486LV00019B/405

9782382268278